3-99

JACQUES LOEB:

HIS SCIENCE AND SOCIAL ACTIVISM AND THEIR PHILOSOPHICAL FOUNDATIONS

JACQUES LOEB:
HIS SCIENCE AND SOCIAL ACTIVISM AND THEIR PHILOSOPHICAL FOUNDATIONS

Charles Rasmussen
and
Rick Tilman

American Philosophical Society
Independence Square • Philadelphia
1998

Memoirs
of the
American Philosophical Society
Held at Philadelphia
For Promoting Useful Knowledge
Volume 229

Library of Congress Card Catalog No.: 95-79390
ISBN: 0-87169-229-5
US ISSN: 0065-9738

PERMISSIONS

The authors thank the following for permission to briefly quote from unpublished materials: Center for American History, University of Texas, Austin, Clarence E. Ayres Papers; Stanford University Archives, George H. Mead and David Starr Jordan Papers; Regenstein Library, University of Chicago. They also thank John C. O'Brien, Editor, for permission to reprint part of "Mechanistic Physiology and Institutional Economics: Jacques Loeb and Thorstein Veblen," *International Journal of Social Economics*, Vol. 19, Nos. 10/11/12 (1992): 235-47.

PREFACE

This book is short in length and limited in scope; it aims simply at explaining the role of one important scientist in society by focusing on his social activism and its philosophical foundations. Its method is primarily textual exegesis and it is Loeb's correspondence which is highlighted rather than his published writings and public speeches. Furthermore, it is his organizational actions and political opinions during the period from 1906 to his death in 1924 that is our primary focus since these were the years of his most intense activism. While he expressed opinions in his correspondence before this time, they concerned a more limited range of issues and actions and thus are less relevant to an understanding of the relationship between his activism and its philosophical foundations. Our concluding chapter pulls the foregoing themes together, relates them to still larger themes, and indicates how this enhances our understanding of the relationship between epistemology, political ideology and social activism.

CHAPTER ONE
JACQUES LOEB AND HIS TIME:
A BIOGRAPHICAL SKETCH

INTRODUCTION

The German-Jewish emigre physiologist Jacques Loeb (1859-1924) was
an unusual scientist in that he was both an important contributor
to biology and an informed and persistent political activist.[1]
Unlike many natural scientists, he did not find it necessary to
relinquish time in the experimental laboratory in order to remain
politically engaged; indeed, he was a formidable and brilliant
researcher who published many books and more than 400 articles
in scientific journals. Although he never won the Nobel Prize for
his contributions to physiology, he was better known and his work
of more lasting value than many of his contemporaries who were
Nobel laureates.[2] Despite the depth of his involvement in science,
he was neither ignorant, naïve or apathetic regarding politics and
social issues—a fact that distinguished him from many of his
fellow scientists.

Loeb's case is made even more unusual because his
metatheoretical, epistemological, and ontological positions were
not only explicitly if loosely stated, but were also integrated with his
political, social and moral philosophy. An avowed atheist and
materialist, he espoused a secular humanism that provided the
underpinnings for an independent radical political outlook.

---

1. The only monographic study of Loeb's life and work is Phillip J. Pauly, *Controlling
Life: Jacques Loeb and the Engineering Ideal in Biology* (New York: Oxford University
Press, 1987). Our brief analysis of Loeb's life, work, and family is based on Pauly,
Louis J. Zanine's, *Mechanism and Mysticism: The Influence of Science on the Thought and
Work of Theodore Dreiser* (Philadelphia: University of Pennsylvania Press, 1993), the
Jacques Loeb Collection, Manuscript Division, Library of Congress, the entries
under Loeb's name in the *Encyclopedia of Philosophy* (New York: The Macmillan
Company and The Free Press, 1967) and *The Dictionary of American Biography* (New
York: Charles Scribner's Sons, 1933); and Robert Duffus's stimulating article
"Jacques Loeb: Mechanist," *Century Magazine,* 108 (1924): 374-83. See also Gerald
Weissman, *The Woods Hole Cantata: Essays on Science and Society,* (New York: Dodd
and Mead, 1985) pp. 1-15.

2. Loeb was nominated for the Nobel Prize in Science or Medicine in 1901, but did
not receive the award.

Loeb attempted both as a social activist and scientist to influence the scientific community, the politically sensitive public, and, ultimately, the underlying population against conservative and reactionary attitudes toward race, ethnicity, poverty, criminality, war and religion. His radical political outlook and his convergent research agenda aimed at undermining theories that rested on prescientific or more often unscientific, that is, pre-Darwinian grounds. These included vitalistic, teleological, introspective, animistic, anthropomorphic, metaphysical and spiritualistic explanations of both the natural and social order. Loeb was most aggressive in his attempts to establish the general principles of an antimetaphysical science of physiology, yet he also believed that his efforts in the scientific laboratory would eventually bear fruit in political and social reform.

Jacques Loeb was born "Isaak" Loeb in 1859 in the town of Mayen, Germany. (He changed his name to Jacques some twenty years later.) Born to a Jewish family, his father was Benedict Loeb, who with his wife Barbara Isay lived in the Rhineland. Loeb's father became a successful merchant and importer who possessed an array of intellectual interests that flavored Jacques' early home life. The elder Loeb was something of a Francophile and developed interests in the sciences which was not uncommon at the time among liberal German intellectuals. Both of Loeb's parents were secular and cultivated; their children were exposed to the ideas of the humanists of eighteenth-century France. The young Loeb read widely in philosophy in his student years, and showed a particular interest in Spinoza, Kant, Schopenhauer and von Hartmann. Early on he developed a plan to study metaphysics as a means of grappling with questions concerning the nature of free will and motivation.

Benedict Loeb, interested in providing his sons with a quality education, sent the young Jacques to the nearby town of Neuwied to attend a school of somewhat higher standards than was available locally. However, the elder Loeb placed his son in the curricular track (Realschule) intended to prepare students for a future in business as opposed to the Gymnasium track which prepared students for continued studies at a university. But family tragedy struck the Loeb children at an early age. Jacques' mother, Barbara, died when he was thirteen years of age, and his father three years later. The children, Jacques and his six year old brother Leo were left in a condition of financial adequacy in terms of a middle-class standard of living, but they were by no means wealthy.

Some time after the death of his father, in 1876 the seventeen-year-old Jacques was sent by his paternal grandfather to work in a bank in Berlin where a relative was employed. While Loeb was now a relatively independent young man with some degree of financial independence, living in the bustling capital with a secure position at a banking house, he was unhappy with the situation; which he later described as "a terrible bore." He left the banking position in less than one year, intent on resuming his studies.

Loeb returned to school at a Jewish Gymnasium in Berlin in order to prepare for entry into a university. He completed this preparatory work in three years and graduated from the Gymnasium in 1880 at the age of twenty-one. It was at this time, following graduation from the Gymnasium in Berlin, that he changed his name from "Isaak Jacques Loeb" to "Jacques Loeb." Loeb immediately entered the University of Berlin to study medicine. However, after only one semester at Berlin, he moved to continue his studies at the University of Munich. During this early portion of his university work, Loeb was exposed to such prominent scientists as Hermann Helmholtz, Carl Voit, C. W. von Kuppfer and Nikolaus Rüdinger. Loeb's early studies tended to channel his interests in the direction of the basic sciences in general and the study of physiology in particular.

In 1881 Loeb moved once again. This time he proceeded to the University of Strassburg to continue his studies under Friedrick Goltz. Goltz himself had joined the Strassburg faculty in 1872; his work focused on the nervous system, and in particular on the brain. He studied the adaptation of animals, particularly dogs, to damage to the cerebral cortex. He would remove significant portions of the cortex from dogs, keep the animals alive for a prolonged period of time after surgery, often for several months, and monitor the processes of adaptation to the cortical trauma. Goltz concluded from his experiments that the contemporary notions of strict localization of function in the cerebral cortex were incorrect and vastly oversimplified. Loeb came to share Goltz's interests and scientific positions; an evolution that could be seen in both his (Loeb's) laboratory work and in his published papers. Loeb completed his medical training in 1884 and in 1885, after being awarded the MD, he left Strassburg to return to Berlin, joining the Berlin Agricultural College to work with physiologist Nathan Zuntz.

Loeb continued to develop his interest and research on the physiological and behavioral effects of brain lesions. He drew two major conclusions; first, that one-sided brain damage had non-symmetrical effects, reducing responses to stimuli on the side opposite the damage; and second, that bilaterally symmetrical damage had global effects on activity levels, increasing or decreasing general activity levels depending on the site of the damage.

In 1886 Loeb moved to a position as assistant in physiology at the medical school at Wurtzburg, working under Professor Adolf Fick. While at Wurtzburg Loeb developed a working relationship with the physiologist Julius Sachs, a scientist whose research was focused on the field of botany. This association with Sachs was to have a profound and long-term influence on Loeb's scientific point of view. Sachs had taken a relatively reductionist approach to understanding plant phenomena. He found that through this approach he could understand many botanical phenomena in terms of basic underlying physical and chemical processes. Sachs was already an eminent botanist and exerted a considerable influence on the young Loeb by introducing him to methods of investigation that lent support to physical and chemical explanations of phenomena observed in the natural world, including phenomena of possible interest to zoologists as well as botanists. Sachs, in turn, was an intellectual descendant of such pioneering mechanists as Emile du Bois-Raymond, Ernst Brucke, Hermann von Helmholtz and Carl Ludwig, all prominent men in the history of the development of science in Germany.

Sachs own work sought (successfully) to demonstrate that phenomena in the plant world could be explained and understood in terms of already known properties of physical and chemical reactions. Sachs' influence upon the young Loeb was immediate. In the former's mechanistic explanations of life phenomena among plants, Loeb perceived an avenue leading not only to an understanding of life processes in animals in general, but also to an explanation of that particular phenomenon labeled "free will." Working under Sachs' guidance, Loeb developed his interests in tropisms (that is, growth or movement of an organism toward or away from a stimulus)—an interest that remained with him for his career. He focused on the underlying variables that controlled the tropistic response, and as his conceptual schema developed , he generalized these basic principles to animal behavior. Building on the concept of tropisms that Sachs conveyed to him during their time together, Loeb broadened the application of this concept to include all vertebrates and this provided an alternative to consciousness as an explanatory variable for understanding behavior.

During his time at Wurtzburg, particularly during 1886-87, Loeb pursued interests in the area he labeled "physiological psychology" and "psychophysics." He studied such topics as human space perception and the interrelationships between physical and mental exertion. While his interest in these areas continued for some years, these pursuits were never at the core of his research agenda. Also during 1887 Loeb published experimental results and theoretical considerations concerning the role of tropisms in animals; in particular he dealt with geotropisms (movement in relation to gravity) and heliotropisms (in relation to sunlight) in insects and their possible role in the behavior of higher animals.

Loeb's lifetime pursuit of a mechanistic explanation of all life phenomena was beginning to take its final mature form. In an 1888 letter to the American philosopher and psychologist William James, Loeb commented:

> Whatever appears to us as innovations, sensations, psychic phenomena, as such are called, I seek to conceive through reducing them—in the sense of modern physics—to the molecular or atomic structure of protoplasm, which acts in a way that is similar to (for example) the molecular structure of the parts of an optically active crystal.[3]

Loeb was also considerably influenced by the Austrian positivists Ernst Mach, a physicist, and the engineer Josef Popper-Lynkeus, the latter an outspoken advocate of social reform. Thus Popper-Lynkeus probably influenced not only Loeb's science but also his developing liberal social beliefs. It was during the 1889-1891 period that Loeb first came under the influence of Ernst Mach. Indeed, in the well-documented study by Phillip Pauly, Mach became the single most important intellectual factor in the development of Loeb's concept of an engineering approach in biology. Loeb initiated his correspondence with Mach in 1887. This prominent scientist was not only a major influence on Loeb's mechanistic and engineering notions for a biology of behavior, his influence reinforced and shaped Loeb's belief in the importance of social issues in his life as a practicing scientist; in this regard, the influence of Mach can be traced through the remainder of Loeb's life. Mach asserted that the scientist must not be seen as a mere explorer of the natural world, but also as a force for social reform and cultural development. Scientists must use their tools to control nature for the general welfare.

It was Mach's contention that topics such as sensation, perception and behavior were simply a part of the biological and physiological functioning of the organism, not some separate realm of mentalistic existence. These processes, sensation, perception and behavior were a result of the same chemical and physical reactions

---

3. Loeb to William James, 10 June 1888, W. James 1892 (509). James, Wm., *The Correspondence of William James,* Skrupskelis, I. K. and Berkeley, E. M. (eds.) (Charlottesville: University Press of Virginia, 1992).

as was the remainder of biology. Mach was a prominent man of science, and his expressions of these views in his correspondence and in his published work reinforced similar views held by the younger scientist, Jacques Loeb. The two never met, but Mach influenced Loeb's entire career.

Disenchanted with the scientific community as he saw it in Wurtzburg in 1888, Loeb returned to Strassburg to take a position as an assistant to Goltz. Still unsettled, however, from 1889 to 1891 he separated his work from the university setting, spending the summers in Zurich and the winters at the Naples Zoological Station in southern Italy. During this period he met a young woman from the United States, Anne Leonard, and in 1890 they were married. In the years to come, the couple had two sons, Leonard, who became a prominent physicist, and Robert, who became a teaching physician at Columbia University Medical School and one daughter, Anne, who after attending Barnard College, became a housewife.

In 1891, Loeb accepted a teaching position at Bryn Mawr College in Pennsylvania. In his book, Gerald Weissman proposes that among Loeb's reasons for emigrating to America, two were prominent: first, the social structure of higher education in Germany made it difficult for Jews to gain success professionally; second, Loeb's early liberal background predisposed him to find intolerable the Prussian orthodoxy prevalent throughout Germany at the time.[4]

Loeb's position at Bryn Mawr College, a newly established Quaker school for women, was obtained in spite of significant reservations on the part of school administrators at the thought of bringing a German Jew to an American Christian college for women. Apparently Loeb obtained the position primarily because it was a seller's market—the institution could locate no other qualified instructors in biology.

In 1892 Loeb accepted a position in physiology at the newly established University of Chicago. Here at last he found a much greater freedom of scientific expression than he had heretofore experienced—at Bryn Mawr or in Germany. The atmosphere among Chicago's faculty was infused with the notion of a progressive improvement in social conditions—a notion with which Loeb was, indeed, quite comfortable. He was a colleague at the University of Chicago of such luminaries as philosophers John Dewey and George Herbert Mead, zoologists Charles Otis Whitman and Charles Benedict Davenport, psychologist James Roland Angell, and sociologist Albion Small. He also came to know and

4. Weissman, *The Woods Hole Cantata,* p. 9.

interact with Thorstein Veblen, the economist.

In 1899, while an associate professor of physiology at the University of Chicago, Loeb developed his technique for inducing artificial parthenogenesis. The occasion provoked quite a stir and considerable controversy among both the scientists and the educated lay public. This development, the induction of artificial parthenogenesis, more than any other single event, established Loeb as a major figure in biology and even in all of science. Loeb was promoted to full professor the following spring and to head professor the year after that. The anatomist Franklin Paine Mall, a colleague at Chicago, raised the serious possibility of Loeb's nomination for the Nobel Prize. Loeb became, in addition to his duties at Chicago, a professor of physiology at Rush Medical College in 1900. In spite of these developments, in the fall of 1902 Loeb accepted a position at the University of California at Berkeley. He departed Chicago for the west coast at the beginning of 1903— lured by the ocean setting for his research using marine animals, the promise of a new laboratory built to his specifications, and a staff of hand-picked assistants. However, his research agenda was somewhat upset by the physical and particularly the economic impact of the great earthquake.

After almost eight years in California, Loeb longed to return to the east. In 1910 he became head of the department of experimental biology at the Rockefeller Institute for Medical Research in New York—he held that position until his death in 1924. During the winter of 1909-1910 Loeb was elected to the National Academy of Sciences, just a few months on the heels of his move to the Rockefeller Institute. Freed from all of the peripheral tasks attendant to a university faculty position, Loeb's productivity increased considerably. He remained an active scientist until his death.

Phillip Pauly summarizes Jacques Loeb's position in science during the years of his prominence:

> By the turn of the century, he had come to symbolize both the appeal and the temptation of open-ended experimentation among biologists in America, and he became the center of scientific and popular controversies over the place of manipulation in the life sciences. Loeb's program influenced a number of the most controversial American life scientists of the next generation, including the behaviorist John B. Watson, the radical geneticist H. J. Muller, and W. J. Crozier, teacher of B. F. Skinner and Gregory Pincus, developer of the birth control pill.[5]

---

5. Pauly, *Controlling Life*, p. 5.

The central thrust of Loeb's research career was an attempt to support his "mechanistic conception of life" which in fact became the title of one of his many books. Louis J. Zanine concludes that Loeb's research agenda was characterized by four major themes: "fertilization and artificial parthenogenesis," "the physico-chemical nature of death," "the study of the brain and central nervous system," and "animal tropisms and instincts."[6]

As we have seen, Loeb's development of the techniques of artificial parthenogenesis marked a major point in his career. Loeb was convinced that the well-known effect of the entry of sperm into the egg initiating the developmental sequence was strictly physico-chemical. He argued heatedly against any vitalistic or animistic explanation for the developmental sequence. On the basis of these convictions, he set upon an extended series of experiments intended to demonstrate the initiation of development without the presence of sperm. He experimented with many mechanical and chemical manipulations and irritants; ultimately, he was able to demonstrate artificial parthenogenesis through application of mild acids and hyperosmotic solutions to sea urchin eggs. When such eggs were returned to a normal sea-water environment, division and development proceeded normally as though the process had been initiated by sperm. By using the process on frogs, which were easier to feed and maintain in the laboratory, he showed that artificial parthenogenesis could produce organisms which were capable of developing to full normal adulthood.

In keeping with his mechanistic explanation for *all* life processes, Loeb saw the duration of the normal lifespan of any given animal as being the amount of time necessary for a series of chemical reactions to reach some end state. Using cold-blooded animals, in particular the fruitfly, he was able to demonstrate successfully that the life span could be manipulated in a perfectly predictable manner by carefully controlling the temperature in which the organisms were maintained. Over a certain range of temperatures, the effect was very nearly linear; that is, at lower temperatures, life span increased.

We discussed earlier the nature of his experiments in manipulating surgically the brains of dogs, and the conclusions he drew from those experiments. The topic of tropisms was one to which he returned again and again. Beginning at the time of his work with Sachs, he demonstrated that the mechanistic tropistic responses shown to exist in plants by Sachs could be generalized to various insect forms and marine animals using a variety of different

---

6. Zanine, *Mechanism and Mysticism*, p. 80.

stimuli such as light, gravity and electric fields. In the case of light, he demonstrated repeatedly that the chemical effect known as the Bunsen-Roscoe law was applicable to living organisms. This law states that the degree of chemical change induced by the presence of light is a product of time (T) and intensity (I), such that $I \times T = C$, with C being a constant value of effect. This relationship, Loeb demonstrated, was equally effective in predicting living behavioral responses to light. (The effect subsequently became known as Block's Law when applied to the psychophysics of human vision.)

CONCLUSION

Although the main thrust of this chapter is to provide the reader with biographical information about Loeb and with a brief summation of his contributions to science, this provides only a backdrop for the analysis of the metatheoretical foundations of his political and social activism. In spite of Loeb's directness and his candor about the epistemological, methodological, and philosophico-political linkages in his own writings, he was occasionally naïve or perhaps even disingenuous regarding these connections. He made several telling comments in discussing a draft of a biography about himself. The draft biography had apparently made reference to some of Loeb's writings as being on the topics of psychology and philosophy. He strongly objected to this characterization, claiming instead that ". . . my contributions consist purely in physico-chemical experiments. I have never indulged in philosophical writings." He argued that when others attempted to explain phenomena in psychological or philosophical terms which he labeled, "old fashioned philosophical, purely speculative views," he, Loeb, simply reformulated the problems in terms of his own laboratory experiments. Therefore he was no longer addressing psychological or philosophical issues but was dealing with the facts of "physico-chemical" science.[7]

It is, of course, commonplace for intellectuals to accuse their personal, methodological, and doctrinal opponents of self-serving motives usually of a material kind; the list of such motives can

---

7. Loeb to Warren Kellog, 26 July 1922. Loeb also wrote: "[Hans] Driesch, who happens to be a personal friend of mine, has never worked along the lines on which I have published, and has never to my knowledge questioned the correctness of any of my results. He, being a vitalist, only believes that it will never be possible to explain life on a purely physico-chemical basis. But this is merely a personal belief of his in which I have not the slightest intention of disturbing him."

include money, power, status, authority, professional aspirations and so forth. Even scientists like Loeb are not immune from such accusations, although he was unusually altruistic in both motives and action. Lily E. Kay has shrewdly commented that:

> In search of patronage, however, most American leaders of pure science did argue for their service role. Their pleas and pledges often projected conflicting images and contradictory purposes: pure research as disinterested knowledge; research as investment in economic growth, human betterment, and political power; objectivity as a mark of professionalization; relevance as a measure of social worth; science as a democratic institution; science as an elite enterprise. Perhaps no scientific figure had embodied and reinforced these contradictions more pointedly than the German émigré Jacques Loeb. America's emblem of pure *wissenschaft*, who, while cleansing biology from the taint of pill-pushing, articulated his intellectual mission in terms of the technological control of life.[8]

Indeed, it is to the relationship between Loeb's scientific endeavors and their philosophic underpinnings on the one hand and his political and social activism on the other that we now turn. In these discussions in chapter two, and indeed in the chapters that follow, the focus of this book is on Jacques Loeb's rather remarkable body of correspondence, particularly for the period 1906 to 1924. Loeb's biography, including his scientific writings and accomplishments have been well documented elsewhere. However, what is also particularly noteworthy in the life of this scientist is the breadth of his community of biologists and physiologists. His intense social activism combined with the prolific nature of his correspondence led to regular communications with politicians, philosophers, union leaders, school teachers, prohibitionists, major authors, government bureaucrats, physicists, military officers, psychologists and housewives. The breadth was remarkable. The names included Theodore Roosevelt, Sigmund Freud, Albert Einstein, William James, Woodrow Wilson, Theodore Dreiser, Julian Huxley, Ernst Mach. Thorstein Veblen, John B. Watson, Oswald Garrison Villard—the list goes on and includes the famous as well as the apparently unknown.

---

8. Lily E. Kay, *The Molecular Vision of Life: Caltech, The Rockefeller Foundation and the Rise of the New Biology* (New York: Oxford University Press, 1993), p. 11.

CHAPTER TWO
LOEB'S PHILOSOPHY AND RESEARCH AGENDA

---◆---

THE INTELLECTUAL FOUNDATIONS OF LOEB'S MECHANISTIC MATERIALISM

The philosophic, moral and scientific antecedents of Jacques Loeb's mechanistic materialism were rooted in the eighteenth century Enlightenment and in Darwinian and post-Darwinian evolutionary theory. Loeb was knowledgeable in regards to his own intellectual pedigree and referred to his ideational antecedents to an unusual extent for a natural scientist. Indeed, in 1916 he dedicated *The Organism as a Whole* to Denis Diderot, the French Encyclopedist, and the other philosophes:

> The book is dedicated to that group of freethinkers, including d'Alembert, Diderot, Holbach, and Voltaire, who first dared to follow the consequences of a mechanistic science—incomplete as it then was—to the rules of human conduct and who thereby laid the foundation of that spirit of tolerance, justice, and gentleness which was the hope of our civilization until it was buried under the wave of homicidal emotion which was swept through the world.[1]

Specifically, Loeb derived from these thinkers the view of man as a machine and to this he added his own view of man as a physico-chemical mechanism emerging during a long evolutionary process which began millions of years ago in a primal soup charged with massive doses of electricity, radioactivity and volcanic heat. He believed that in this environment, organic material had ultimately developed from inorganic compounds and he was convinced that this process of evolution, including humankind's role in it, could be explained scientifically. He reached this conclusion before Alexander Oparin and J. B. S. Haldane did (1924-1936), a point worth mentioning since their findings constitute a landmark in the history of science.

Loeb possessed a considerable knowledge of the history of science, but his view was characteristic of a grandchild of the

---

1. Jacques Loeb, *The Organism as a Whole* (New York and London: G. P. Putnam's Sons, 1916), p. VIII.

11

Enlightenment with the particular mindset that results from constant recitation of the litany of the Age of Reason. To illustrate this point, he asserted that the Aristotelian view was of a universe created to center on man. Loeb saw that such a philosophy led to the belief that, as a result of the grand design of the creator of such a universe, the world as it is, is the world as it should be; this view, espoused by the church, combined with a "predatory system of economics" produced the harsh, impoverished and brutal world of the Middle Ages. Three individuals, Copernicus, Galileo, and later Darwin, introduced ideas which were seminal in breaking with this suffocating tradition. First, Copernicus and Galileo objected to the notion that the physical universe centered on and revolved around man. Building on the work of T. H. Huxley and Ernst Haeckel, Darwin attacked the idea that life on earth was also a result of a master plan. To the distress of the church, Darwin announced that life forms were the result of selective pressures of the environment combined with chance variations in individual characteristics;[2] the outcome of evolution was neither bad nor good, simply the outcome of competing forces. This particular view of history, especially European history, portrayed science and reason as the liberators of mankind; Loeb was undoubtedly egocentric enough to believe he was making a lasting contribution to human emancipation through his own scientific efforts. His work on tropisms and colloid chemistry was viewed by him as a means for undermining both religious

---

2. Ibid., p. 346. Whatever reservations Loeb had regarding Darwinism and the theory of natural selection probably had to do primarily with the difficulty of quantification since otherwise Loeb was a defender and, at times, a bellicose supporter of evolutionary biology. This included the aggressive articulation of Darwinism to lay people to aid them in differentiating between natural selection on the one hand and Lamarckian inheritance of acquired characteristics on the other. To illustrate, he wrote to Eustace Conway, 31 January 1917, in New York City to explain that:

> It is perfectly true that through muscular activity the muscles of an individual can be increased in size, but unfortunately this increase is not transmitted to the offsprings. Even if it were true that a certain part of the brain, if not used, would undergo atrophy—a statement for which we have not the slightest proof and which is probably untrue—yet it would not mean that the offspring of a person with such a partially atrophied brain would inherit the same atrophy. Our present knowledge tells us that such partial variations are not transmitted to the offspring. The son of a father who has never taken any exercise and whose muscles have never been developed will for that reason not have any weaker muscles than if he were the son of a pugilist or some other type of athlete.

Like many Western scientists Loeb, after an initial period of uncertainty, or perhaps even flirtation with the Lamarckian doctrine of the inheritance of acquired traits, firmly embraced Darwin's natural selection.

superstition in the community at large and prescientific assumptions still rampant among biologists and chemists. In this sense, he may have seen himself as a worthy successor to the great figures in science named above.

Loeb expended much intellectual capital trying to discredit vitalism and entelechy among natural scientists, ideas which were much more pervasive during his lifetime than currently. Although for a time many critics anticipated the death or at least the ebbing of such tendencies they underwent a resurgence, instead, and he thus felt obligated to combat them. He believed that several obstacles to a modern mechanistic science of life were due as much to the activities of some scientists as they were to religion and other forces outside the realm of science.

As part of his plan to combat prescientific modes of thinking Loeb strongly espoused the principal of tracing complex processes back to underlying simple reactions or combinations of simple reactions; he argued that the more complex patterns of response observable in animals may be better understood by examining simpler reactions such as tropisms in plants, which, in turn, could be understood in terms of underlying "physicochemical laws." He took to task other scientists such as Ludwig Haberlandt, and Francis Darwin (both botanists) for attempting to do just the reverse, that is, tracing simple plant reactions back to the more complex processes observable in animals. He was particularly severe in his criticism of some scientists for going so far as to endow plants with "sense organs," "intelligence," and even a "soul." Sarcastically, he countered with the suggestion that molecules and ions be so imbued.[3] It is thus interesting to note that some of Loeb's writing on these subjects resembled that of his friend and former colleague Thorstein Veblen in terms of its mockery and satire.

Although Loeb was strongly critical of vitalistic efforts to explain biological processes he recognized that much remained to be explained. He attacked the vitalist notion that for each organism there exists a plan or design and a guiding force to carry out such a plan in determining the form that the organism will take as it develops from the egg. This notion removed the study of the factors determining the form of a developing organism from the realm of science, in particular from the fields of physics and chemistry. While giving credit to the Darwinian concepts of natural selection as being free of such notions of a guiding force, he felt that the theory as it

---

3. Jacques Loeb, "The Significance of Tropisms for Psychology," *The Popular Science Monthly,* 79 (August, 1911): 122.

stood lacked a foundation in physics and chemistry, areas he felt were essential to an understanding of life processes.[4] Loeb's assertion that Darwin's theory lacked a foundation in chemistry anticipated today's rather well developed concepts such as the work of James D. Watson and Francis Crick describing the molecular structure of deoxyribonucleic acid (DNA).

Loeb was relentless in his criticism of non-materialist explanations of biological phenomena whether they took the form of vitalism or some related approach which might variously be labeled "entelechy," "teleological," "spiritualistic," "purposive," "guiding force," "metaphysical," *"elan vital"* or other. Although these explanations of biological organisms and processes were similar in Loeb's view, their proponents often claimed they were conceptually different. This undoubtedly complicated Loeb's task in discrediting them because he had to combat a wide array of nonphysicalistic explanations produced by thinkers from disciplines as divergent as chemistry, philosophy, biology, physics and theology. In Loeb's correspondence, his favorite opponent was the French philosopher Henri Bergson whose book *Creative Evolution* (1910) was widely read and influential and who knew enough of Loeb's anti-metaphysical position to denounce it. In his published work, however, Loeb focused on the work of scientists such as the Frenchman Claude Bernard. What further complicated Loeb's task was that some of the purveyors of nonmaterialist science were themselves very competent scientists of stature in their own fields and Bernard was one such man. Loeb stated that while Bernard was willing to take a mechanistic position as regards the understanding of individual processes in the development of the organism, he insisted on using, to Loeb's exasperation, the notion of a "directive force" as an explanatory concept in understanding the determinants of the final complete form that an organism would take as it developed from a single undifferentiated egg. Loeb charged, quite accurately, that Bernard denied the possibility of explaining the "harmonious organism" in terms of mechanistic processes. While individual life processes could be explained mechanistically, Bernard claimed that only an outside "directive force" could bring these individual processes together with the orchestration necessary to produce the complete organism. Loeb found Bernard's ideas "incomprehensible" except perhaps being a result of the latter's ignorance of the most recent scientific evidence.[5]

Thus, even in criticizing Bernard, Loeb recognized that the

---

4. Loeb, *The Organism as a Whole*, pp. V-VI.

5. Ibid., pp. 2-4.

immature development of the biological sciences was partly to blame for the Frenchman's deficiencies; but since important conceptual and theoretical gaps had now been filled, there was no adequate rationale for the persistence of resistance to materialist explanations of natural phenomena. Indeed, in Loeb's view, his own work on sea urchins was one of the means by which the gaps were filled.

The persistence of a variety of anthropomorphic and teleological arguments often drawn from philosophical theology made Loeb's task difficult. For every time he located the "enemy," it was a fleeting, transient identification because of the diversity of forms in which such analyses were clothed. Two such arguments Loeb attacked were those based on "design" and the *perpetuum mobile.* The argument for the existence of God based on design has a long history in Christian theology and apologetics and, despite the devastating attack on it by David Hume in his *Dialogues on Natural Religion* in the eighteenth century, it continued to exert influence on scientists into the twentieth century. Loeb used a different strategy than Hume but his analysis was equally negative. He suggested that the obvious purposefulness of animal instincts and animal "will" is more apparent than real. He cited physics as a parallel case; prior to more recent concepts in astronomy, it was "obvious" that the movements of the heavenly bodies centered on man and that there was plan and purpose behind those movements. Later developments in celestial mechanics (Copernicus, Galileo, Newton) made such notions of purpose evaporate. By the same token, Loeb felt that an understanding of the physical and chemical processes underlying instinct will make "the assumption of design [become] superfluous."[6]

Loeb's intellectual candor compelled him to admit that he could not fully or adequately explain existing life forms and that, as yet, no scientists were able to make life in a laboratory. Nevertheless, he continued to criticize nonmaterialist explanations of biological phenomena. Loeb declined to accept the assertion that living matter had an existence entirely separate from non-living matter. He suggested the possibility that life had been produced from non-living matter during an earlier stage of the planet's development and as a result of naturally occurring forces such as lightning, radioactivity, and volcanic activity. At the same time that these discussions concerning the production of living matter took place, there were, in some circles, discussions of the creation of a perpetual motion machine. Some scientists declared such a

6. Ibid., pp. 253-54.

creation an impossibility while others declared the creation of living matter to be a parallel and equally impossible task. Loeb deftly separated the two notions, pointing out that while a perpetual motion machine was impossible due to the first law of thermodynamics, there was as yet no known natural law which prevented the artificial creation of living from non-living matter. He asserted that while neither the spontaneous generation of life nor the creation of life from non-living matter had ever been observed this did "not prove that a synthesis of living from dead matter is impossible under any conditions."[7]

Loeb may or may not have suspected the existence of genetic coding; nevertheless, the discovery of DNA lay far in the future. Much of the scientific data and theory that would have strengthened his case against the metaphysicians of science was not available to him. But Loeb mustered what scientific findings he could as he made a systematic effort throughout his mature years as a scientist to discredit his ideological foes. For example, in 1916 he very neatly anticipated modern concepts of DNA as the master code for various proteins whose timely production and release serve in turn as the causative agents for various bodily functions and structures, when he wrote "[If the egg contains the plan for the embryo,] we can imagine the Mendelian factors as giving rise to specific substances which go into circulation and start or accelerate different chemical reactions in different parts of the embryo, and thereby call forth the finer details characteristic of the variety and the individual." So Loeb asserts that, rather than requiring an external master design and a force by which to execute such a design, the egg contains within itself the plan of its own future form; he felt his own work on artificial parthenogenesis provided strong support for his conclusions, involving as it did the production of a normal adult organism without the presence of a sperm. Furthermore, he asserted that this mechanistic conception of life is valid even in the absence of a theory of evolution, or indeed, in the absence of evolution itself.[8] In summation, then, Loeb's idealized version of the evolutionary process and the most appropriate scientific approach to its study was rooted in the cosmology and metaphysics of a reductionist materialism.

Throughout much of his academic career Loeb focused his efforts on convincing his reading audience that a mechanistic materialism would ultimately prove to be the basis for a scientific

7. Ibid., pp. 38-9.

8. Ibid., pp. 6-10.

explanation of the evolution and behavior of all biological organisms including humankind. At first, this meant a research emphasis on tropisms, but later it came to mean colloid chemistry also. As time passed, Loeb's research activity became focused almost exclusively on the physical chemistry of colloids. He stated emphatically that the physical and chemical laws of the actions of colloids were applicable to the general array of phenomena of interest to the physiologists; all of life can be understood, he asserted, in terms of colloidal behavior. He concluded that general physiology will reach its full potential only when a quantitative theoretical model of colloidal behavior is at hand, and that "this theory will become one of the foundations on which modern physiology will have to rest."[9] Loeb concluded that at some future stage in the development of the biological sciences "man the machine" would become an empirically verifiable reality not a mere figment of a researcher's imagination.

Since he carefully kept abreast of developments not only in his own field of physiology but also in chemistry and physics, it is not surprising that he drew insights from all three as he continued to work toward the achievement of his goal which was a more sophisticated mechanistic materialism than any which existed. The understanding of the particulate nature of matter had reached such a level of sophistication that it became possible for physical chemists to determine the exact number of molecules in any given weight of a material. From this growing body of knowledge in the physical sciences, Loeb saw that ultimately all physical phenomena could be explained in terms of atoms, molecules, charges, interactions, and combinations. Thus far in the chain of his logic there was no conflict with many of the scientists who were his contemporaries. To this, Loeb added his fundamental assumption that life itself could be understood in terms of the physical and chemical principles then being uncovered; he concluded that "since there is no discontinuity between the matter constituting the living and non-living world the goal of biology can be expressed in the same way."[10] This was, of course, a powerful and compelling assertion and one which drew immediate and violent rebuttal from both within and without the scientific establishment.

Going well beyond basic life processes Loeb's research objectives clearly involved laying the ground work for a mechanistic explanation of human behavior and mental processes (or "psychic

---

9. Jacques Loeb, *Proteins and the Theory of Colloidal Behavior* (New York: McGraw-Hill, 1924), pp. 370-71.

10. Loeb, *The Organism as a Whole,* p. 1.

phenomena," the term more commonly used during that era). Expanding on his views concerning living and non-living matter, he argued that psychic phenomena were also subject to explanations based on principles set forth by the physical and chemical sciences; that is to say, mental experiences and even "free will" are simply the manifestations of physical and chemical processes taking place within the body—processes which were becoming well understood at the time. These were the same "physico-chemical" processes being used to explain comparatively basic phenomena observed in non-living material. Loeb simply argued that, there being no fundamental difference between living and non-living matter, the underlying physical and chemical processes of say, acids, bases and salt solutions on one hand, and mental processes such as memory and decision making on the other hand are identical. He recognized that many individuals, among them many scientists, would take issue with such ideas. Loeb strongly disagreed with the notion that ultimately "truly psychical" phenomena were not amenable to physico-chemical explanations. He argued that it was high time that science embark on a physico-chemical analysis of mental processes and that the methods be the same as those used for the investigation of the most simple processes found in non-living material. Loeb recognized that not only was there resistance to his mechanistic materialism among natural scientists, but that this philosophy was not convincing to many social scientists either. He pointed out that, just as he had argued in several articles beginning in 1888, "will" in simpler organisms was nothing more than the action of combinations of tropisms; and that his reductive principles could also be applied to the problems confronted by psychologists and sociologists.[11]

The frustration Loeb must have felt at times in conveying his message to the recalcitrant is occasionally evident in his satirical jibes at the unconverted. Mostly, however, he was even-tempered and impersonal in his published work, however much he let his feelings betray him in his correspondence with friends and colleagues. His research agenda was often carefully and forcefully stated. Beginning with an analysis of very simple life forms, he saw movement as simply a matter of orientation of the body in relation to various external stimuli such as light, electric fields, chemical concentrations and gravity. These organisms are often symmetrical in both form and chemical sensitivity and directional shifts in movement or growth can be seen as simple responses that reorient the organism in such a way as to produce or reacquire symmetrical

---

11. Loeb, "The Significance of Tropisms for Psychology," p. 105.

stimulation by external stimuli, as when a growing plant root is affected by gravity or certain aquatic animals swim toward light. He saw the more complex activities of higher animal forms as being nevertheless based on more intricate combinations of the same underlying physical and chemical processes. A scientific psychology, or in his terms a "comparative psychology," would eventually eclipse the "speculative psychology" of the time; this new scientific psychology would enter the realm of biologists because of their greater familiarity with the principles of physico-chemical processes and their training in the scientific methods necessary for their further investigation.[12] Thus the new scientific psychology will join the other sciences in moving toward Ernst Mach's ideal of an active science engineering the environment for the common social good.

Nor was Loeb averse to speculating on the application of laboratory work to both psychiatry and ethics. Indeed, regarding the former he once wrote that:

> I believe that the investigation of the conditions which produce tropisms may be of importance for psychiatry. If we can call forth in an animal otherwise indifferent to light by means of an acid a heliotropism which drives it irresistibly into a flame; if the same thing can be brought about by means of a secretion of the reproductive glands; then we have given, I believe, a group of facts, within which the analogies necessary for psychiatry can be experimentally called forth and investigated.[13]

He also attempted to bridge the gap between mental states and ethics when he observed that just as Pavlov induced biochemical activity (salivation) in organisms (dogs), as a result of external physical stimuli (bells), so also the notion of an "idea" may be a series of biochemical changes within the body. The process of salivation becomes a fixed response to the stimulus. By the same token, the notion of human self-sacrifice, Loeb felt, may be conceptualized not as an ethical decision but "that under the influence of certain ideas chemical changes, for instance, internal secretions within the body" may result in absolute stimulus control of behavior.[14] Clearly, Loeb had come to believe that an adequate materialist explanation of human behavior would have important consequences both in the development of psychiatry and in the social sciences. His speculation did not end there, however, for he

---

12. Ibid., p. 124.

13. Ibid., p. 125.

14. Ibid.

saw with considerable prescience its implications for ethical theory and the study of moral issues.

Loeb more or less continuously attempted to link his scientific work with current political and social issues. Some of his commentary in this regard falls into the realm of political psychology for he was very interested in the degree to which autocratic regimes manipulated public opinion and duped the masses into submissive behavior contrary to their own self-interest. It is interesting to note that he found a physiological basis for political indoctrination. Loeb anticipated the findings of modern polygraphy when he speculated that words and phrases could induce measurable physiological changes within the body which in turn induce states of passion. Polygraphy is based on the notion that phrases ("Did you murder your wife") may result in chemical secretions (adrenaline) which in turn cause emotional and physiological changes (anxiety and heart acceleration). Just as these phrases exert some control over internal physiological states, Loeb likewise concludes that, "Humans with such a reduced number of degrees of freedom of will can easily be led in that single direction which corresponds to the single degree of freedom left open to them."[15] He acknowledged that, "it is not necessary that the influence of phrases should in all cases be explained in this way."[16] Loeb stated that individual choice was drastically constrained by social circumstances and, more importantly, by physiological processes within the brain and body; to be logically consistent he should totally deny freedom of will which suggests the statement above is a mere concession to expediency.

As will be discussed in more detail in the next chapter, Loeb believed, too, that the autocratic, reactionary elements responsible for the Great War had for decades before its outbreak disseminated racist propaganda of a highly unscientific nature. This had created an environment in which militarism, racism and imperialism could flourish. Continuing the above discussions of the ability of phrases to control and restrict human behavior, Loeb observed, during the early portions of World War I, that the ". . . latest addition to the

---

15. Jacques Loeb, "Freedom of the Will and War," *New Review*, 2 (1914): 633. He also asserts: The question is: What induces the masses, even the Socialists, to become the dupes of these destructive elements? For there can be no doubt that in the present war the masses in Germany, Austria-Hungary, France and possibly even in Russia went to war with amazing unanimity. This is generally explained psychologically. The writer will try to substitute a kindred but somewhat more physiological explanation. Ibid., p. 631.

16. Ibid., p. 633.

store of phrases by which all degrees of freedom of will in the masses can be suppressed except the one of rushing to the front is that of 'Racial Superiority' and 'Racial Antipathy.'" Loeb thus argued that "militaristic government[s]" prepare for war by the process of conditioning their people with these phrases and others such as "peace without honor" and "defend their country" until every "degree of freedom" of action has been removed except that of fighting. When this has been successfully accomplished, said government will inevitably "blunder into war." He argued that "the people" must maintain an awareness of this potential for manipulation and by so doing, avoid the consequences."[17] In Loeb's analysis, then, "freedom of the will" is not merely a physiologically conditioned state of mind; it is also a propagandistically constrained social process which strips the individual of alternative courses of thinking and acting until at last only one "choice" is possible.

MONISM AND THE METAPHYSICS OF MATERIALISM

Loeb was very aware of the political and ideological struggle in which he was involved. He was also sensitive to the negative relationship between the scientific and materialist viewpoint on the one hand and reactionary politics, religious superstition, imperialism, racism and war on the other hand. Loeb saw himself

---

17. Ibid., p. 636. He argues: The attitude of the French and German Socialists has been a surprise to many. Closer analysis will show that we must judge them mildly in spite of the irreparable harm they have done to the belief that through Socialism humanity will be free from war. We have pointed out that the phrase used by the German (and in all probability also by the Russian) press is that this is a "race war"—Teutonism v. Slavism. The Socialists had learned enough not to be deceived by the clamoring for expansion of trade; they were also probably prepared to resist a desire of the Nationalists for territorial expansions, but they had not yet recognized the danger of the phrase: "racial superiority"—it is indeed a mere phrase, unsupported by any scientific fact and contradicted by the laws of heredity. Talent and, in all appearance, moral qualities, run in families and strains, independently of race. The hereditary characters are transmitted as a rule independently of each other, and with a black skin the highest talent and the highest moral powers may be combined, while a complete absence of both may accompany a white skin. As long as the Socialist worship at the shrine of "racial antipathy" and "racial superiority," as many of them actually do, they will continue to be an unreliable factor in the process of civilization. It is a great pity that the Socialists get their information on heredity—the laws of which have only become clear in the last decade—either from the older scientific literature or from purely literary writers who are also responsible for the ideas of racial superiority which dominate Germany today.
Ibid., pp. 634-35.

21

as an active participant in a vast conflict of ideas of great moral and doctrinal import. He viewed some of his own work, particularly his collection of essays, *The Mechanistic Conception of Life,* as being aimed primarily at the advancement of his own point of view in this struggle rather than breaking new scientific ground. He referred to this collection as "a piece of campaign literature." Loeb feared a period of growing vitalistic reaction against the progress of scientific materialism and cited negative European influences, particularly from French and German exchange professors. He followed the speeches and pronouncements of the vitalists, referring in letters to their comments about "the medieval fanaticism of certain monists."[18] Loeb was, of course, referring to the attacks on himself and his philosophy of monism which incorporated the premises of mechanistic materialism among its ontological and epistemological axioms.

Although Loeb became committed to a research program that would ultimately explain mind solely in terms of physical chemistry, he was not always optimistic that this was an achievable goal in the short run. Indeed, his correspondence with other scientists, in particular, makes it clear that he was well aware that his involvement was in nothing more than the most basic research. As time advanced, his research became more focused on work which he hoped would lead to a theory of colloids. He was convinced that the future of biology in general was inextricably linked to an understanding of the physical and chemical processes of colloids which would enhance understanding of the mechanistic processes of life itself.[19]

Evidently, after Loeb turned his research interests away from tropismatic behavior to physical chemistry, he began to encounter serious opposition to his work from other chemists, particularly Europeans. On 4 September 1922 he wrote to Albert Einstein:

> It would have been a great satisfaction to me if I had a chance to bring some of my results before the physical chemists, since I have a very limited audience in this country and since in Germany they are not familiar with literature published during the war years. In addition, the opposition on the part of the majority of the biologists to any application of physical chemistry to biological problems, and the opposition of the old-fashioned type of colloid chemists like Wolfgang Ostwald, prevent the dissemination of these facts in German literature.[20]

18. Loeb to Wolfgang Ostwald, no date.

19. Loeb to Joseph McCabe, 22 December 1921.

20. Loeb to Albert Einstein, 4 September 1992.

Loeb's monism and materialism underlay both his scientific and political activities and, it is important to note, those scientists most aware of this were able to detect the doctrinal tendencies of his work. Some, like his friends Albert Einstein and Thorstein Veblen, shared most of his ideological proclivities; yet others who were politically and philosophically more conservative were skeptical of his research agenda and repelled by his radical political views.

It should be noted that Loeb well understood his own intellectual antecedents, that is, the historical and cultural roots of mechanistic materialism. In his view, the origins were to be found in the French Encyclopedists and other freethinkers of the Age of Reason. Diderot, D'Alembert, Holbach and Helvetius were believed by Loeb to be the earliest expressions of his viewpoint and he occasionally alluded to them in his correspondence as at least rudimentary sources of his epistemology and ontology. Probably few scientists of his time were literate enough in European intellectual history to understand the modern origins of the secular materialist perspective, especially its antimetaphysical axioms.

Reference should also be made to Loeb's radical behaviorism and environmental determinism because this clearly had a direct bearing on his political and social philosophy and his attitudes toward social reform. Indeed, he warned against confusing hereditary effects with purely environmental ones in advising those who used statistics to understand poverty and social deviancy.

That Loeb experienced difficulties in demonstrating the relationship between his own brilliant laboratory experiments on lower forms of animal life and the nature and behavior of human beings is undeniable. Nevertheless, he was determined that through his extraordinarily ambitious research program and others that would develop out of it, mind could be explained through physico-chemical processes. Loeb never claimed that he could adequately explain the formation of ideational patterns in the brain of Homo sapiens through his own experiments or those of others. But he apparently believed, at least in principle, that the cerebral processes which produced thought would eventually be explained by physical chemistry.

EPISTEMOLOGY, SCIENTIFIC METHOD, AND THE STATE OF BIOLOGY

Loeb was more or less continuously in a state of conflict with other individuals and groups holding opposing political, ideological and scientific ideas. Sometimes these conflicts smoldered beneath the surface for years before they erupted into overt disagreement; more often, however, Loeb was likely to inform his opponents politely but firmly that he disagreed with them; on many occasions he simply ignored his differences with critics because he believed they were not adequately prepared scientifically or intellectually to be taken too seriously. This was especially true in his dealings with certain other biological scientists whom he considered incompetent to deal with the major issues at hand. However, it was not the mere flaunting of his prowess as a scientist that was at issue or the exercise of his ego; instead, as he put it:

> We cannot expect to explain the physico-chemical side of life phenomena until we know more about the elementary physico-chemical processes than we do now. The usual type of twaddle in which many physiologists and biologists indulge may have a market value but does not lead us any further in science.[21]

Loeb believed that many of his opponents and critics in biology were inspired by something other than intellectual detachment and the objectivity that underlies the love of scientific truth. He thought this was particularly true of those who held negative views of his work on tropisms. He felt that many individuals attracted to the study of tropisms entered such work with preconceived vitalistic notions about the special nature of living matter. Beginning with such a bias, and accompanied by what Loeb felt were often less than adequate experimental skills, it was an easy step for these individuals to conclude that animal behavior cannot be fully explained in terms of the cause and effect world of physical and chemical laws. Loeb named specific individuals, such as the biologists H. S. Jennings, and Samuel O. Mast as being part of a reactionary movement resisting the theory of tropisms because it threatened their own prejudices.[22] Loeb thus viewed the opponents of his work on tropisms as conservatives with metaphysical axes to grind who lacked the motivation and training to pass judgment on his accomplishments. He categorized opponents of a tropismatic theory of behavior as being either outside the realm of modern biology or as biologists who lacked training and experience in physical chemistry.[23]

However, more than any biological scientist Loeb's *bête noire* was

---

21. Loeb to Richard Goldschmidt, 28 January 1921.

22. Loeb to Sakyo Kanda, 12 February 1912.

23. Loeb to M. H. Baega, 3 October 1912.

the French philosopher Henri Bergson (1859-1941), the leading European exponent of vitalism. Loeb saw Bergson as a mystic, and worse, even as a charlatan. In a letter to a friend dated 1917 he called Bergson "a medicine man," a telling and derogatory comment at the time. While on a lecture tour in the United States, Bergson denounced Loeb and his ideas as dangerous; Loeb speculated that the cause of Bergson's ire was that he, Loeb, had poked fun at Bergson in an article published in the *Yale Review*, "Mechanistic Science and Metaphysical Romance." But Loeb was less playful and a bit more intense when he came across the occasional scientist who supported Bergson. In a letter he commented, "When I see that even biologists take a man like Bergson seriously, I wonder whether it is not a great pity that humanity has so completely lost the crude vestige of its simian origin."[24] We may assume that Loeb was suggesting that such biologists should be in trees swinging by their tails.

Bergson's writings and ideas elevated him to a position of prominence and some popularity; his admirers included such luminaries of the day as William James. Bergson's philosophy was a dualist, vitalist notion of creative free choice which stoutly rejected such ideas as mechanism and materialism. He can be described as an evolutionist but not in the mechanist-materialist manner envisaged by Charles Darwin. Rather, he proposed a "creative evolution" guided by a creative force or *élan vital,* a stream of consciousness in all matter. This force guides evolution as it moves with divine purpose toward a higher goal of human consciousness; thus he argued that there is a purpose to evolution. Bergson posited a worldview of existence which was not subject to scientific verification or to rational analysis. Intuition, he argued, is the only source of absolute knowledge, while science, mathematics, and logic provide only "relative knowledge." Jacques Loeb, of course, took issue with all of these notions. However, the Bergson position with which he most frequently and most heatedly disagreed was the assertion that the universe is composed of two fundamentally different forms of existence, inorganic versus organic, that is to say, nonliving matter versus life. Loeb, throughout his career, argued that both living and nonliving matter obey the same laws of physics and chemistry, indeed that life itself is simply a sequence of chemical reactions, and the duration of life is the time required for those chemical reactions to be completed.

As was his inclination, Loeb fought with the vitalists whenever the opportunity presented itself. He gave speeches, in the U.S. and

24. Loeb to Edwin Ray Lankester, 9 July 1917.

in Europe, in which he vigorously attacked the vitalist position and presented an alternative which he described as "a kind of programme of the mechanistic conception of life." He sent copies of such addresses to friends and fellow anti-vitalists and urged their circulation to the widest possible audience. He labeled active anti-vitalists as "fighters" and bemoaned those times when their voices were not heard with what he felt was adequate frequency and force.[25]

In summary Loeb believed that his work on tropisms was not adequately understood by critics because of their lack of familiarity with physical chemistry. Many scientists of the time, he felt, were burdened by inadequate training in scientific method. As he once put it, these individuals who "had *only* a morphological or a medical training, are not familiar with the principles of scientific analysis." He continues harshly, "Their life is on the whole wasted as far as the progress of science is concerned" and concludes that these scientists "may contribute to the classification of ants . . . or diseases," but they are "unable to contribute anything" to the advancement of a mechanistic science of life.[26]

Loeb was philosophically sophisticated enough to recognize that in the long run, at least, it matters greatly both to intellectual elites and to the common man how the relationship between science, religion and morality is construed. He had a powerful sensitivity to the view that the scientific and religious realms are simply not compatible with each other in that no coherent epistemological position can accommodate both. In Loeb's view one must ultimately give way to the other and he had little doubt about which would ultimately triumph. In a letter to a friend, he discussed the visit of the physiologist J. B. S. Haldane of Oxford University to Yale where the latter delivered a series of lectures. Loeb was critical of Haldane's concept of "The New Physiology"; Haldane argued that, after years of effort, the mechanistic approach to physiology, using the techniques of physics and chemistry had accomplished nothing and therefore it was time to return to a vitalistic approach to the subject. With thinly veiled sarcasm, Loeb concludes, "He did not come near the Rockefeller Institute [where Loeb and his research laboratories were located] to my knowledge; I suppose he visited the physiological laboratories at the various theological seminaries, which agree more with his conception of physiology."[27]

---

25. Loeb to Georges Bohn, 6 November 1911.

26. Ibid., 11 October 1912.

27. Loeb to Hardolph Wasteneys, 1 November 1915.

Loeb was also strongly aware that his empiricist epistemology and materialist metaphysics had political as well as moral and philosophical implications—implications which his scientific and doctrinal opponents sensed in their rejection of his views. Even socialists like his acquaintance William English Walling, who generally agreed with Loeb on matters political and epistemological, had doubts about his refusal to establish parameters for his scientific materialism whose burgeoning claims threatened to take on the form of an intellectual imperialism. One of their exchanges illuminates their disagreement over epistemological boundaries, Walling wrote:

> Of course I read your *Das Leben*—on the train within an hour of the time I got it. What the world would mechanical materialism be seems to me only the outer framework of our life, or its ultimate basis. I do not see why one cannot accept everything you say and still retain everything that is valuable in a sane common-sense psychology. In the same way, I have never found that the economic interpretation of history interfered with the most subtle spiritual interpretations. I mean those reached starting from the opposite standpoint. But in so far as the latter contradicted the former they prove to be false.[28]

Loeb replied to Walling with whom he had apparently exchanged books that:

> I read your book with great interest but as you might expect I do not quite agree with it. I am of the opinion that science is and has to remain the solid ground on which we stand, no less for the conduct of human affairs than for anything else. If we leave the solid ground we are no longer master of our judgment or destiny. You know that Bergson is hailed by the reactionaries as the man who has freed France from science and has allowed it to return to the ideas of the church. We cannot develop any future society except on the basis of facts, since otherwise we never know whether we are right or wrong, and we shall fall into the same errors which have made life in the middle ages impossible and are making it pretty nearly so today. The trouble with all the reactionaries is that they do not use science as their basis to conduct and their aims.[29]

Loeb believed that other fashionable intellectual and theoretical currents, although not specifically religious, were

28. William English Walling to Loeb, no date.

29. Loeb to William English Walling, 10 May 1913.

close enough to serve as ersatz-religion, and must therefore be combated. Late in life and physically enfeebled, and thus less combative, he was still alert to the dangers latent in such beliefs and vigorous in his opposition to such doctrines as vitalism. In a letter dated May 1921, just three years before his death, Loeb resisted an invitation to engage in a debate on vitalism. He stated his belief that vitalism was simply another expression of that group of religious and quasi-religious beliefs which includes spiritualism and occultism. Discussions with individuals holding such beliefs are to no avail and basically a waste of time and energy. He had long since concluded that mechanistic principles provided the only productive framework or guide within which science could efficiently proceed. He asserts that, "Science will develop on the basis of mechanistic principles and through quantitative methods and neither vitalism nor occultism will prevent that development." He rejects the invitation to discuss the topic of vitalism with the statement, "I have ceased to take an interest in this problem."[30]

That Loeb's epistemological views were closely linked with scientific method and that he viewed his social and political philosophy as an outgrowth of both of the former is evident in his writings. In a piece of correspondence to Richard Palmer dated December 1922, he attempted to further differentiate the mechanistic and antimechanistic viewpoints. He asserted that the mechanistic approach to the study of life processes is inherently reductionistic; phenomena such as heliotropism and regeneration can best be understood and manipulated by means of the underlying processes of physics and chemistry. Those who felt compelled to take anti-mechanistic often vitalistic, positions were led astray by two factors. In the first place they were ignorant of the principles of physics and chemistry that had been established by that time. In the second place, those few anti-mechanists who had been trained in physics and chemistry were insufficiently knowledgeable of the ongoing nature of scientific progress. That is, when faced with a life phenomenon which was not yet amenable to mechanistic explanation, they felt compelled to turn to vitalistic explanations rather than accept the ambiguity of an as yet unexplained phenomenon.[31]

Perhaps Loeb's most explicit attack on vitalism and related doctrines came in correspondence with Joseph M. Park. In a letter dated February 1915, Loeb attacked "permanent armchair

---

30. Loeb to Eugenio Rignano, 23 May 1921.

31. Loeb to Richard Palmer, 2 December 1922.

scientists" as the only remaining members of the scientific establishment who continue to argue that nonliving material differs from living material in that the latter is infused with or characterized by a "vital force." He contrasted these "armchair scientists" with "laboratory men" who due to their experiences in experimental settings have advanced beyond vitalistic notions. The vitalists, Loeb asserted, base their conclusions on the fact that there remain in the biological sciences so many phenomena for which there is no ready explanation; they believe that that which is without explanation today will remain in such a state permanently. In this missal, Loeb thus argues passionately that biology is a progressive, advancing field with new findings providing explanations for previously mysterious phenomena. About these phenomena he concludes, "Science has not yet been able to imitate these phenomena artificially and hence they belong to the unsolved problems. But this does not mean that they are problems which can never be solved."[32]

Loeb laid considerable stress on the need for a greater understanding of the ethos of science and scientific method if greater social progress were to occur. Like his acquaintance John Dewey, he emphasized the role of the educational system in bringing this about. He blamed "theologists, philosophers, and the rest of the unscientific writers" for creating a situation in which the average reader was unable to differentiate unsubstantiated assertions from experimentally derived fact, or as Loeb put it "between certainty and mere vague talk." The solution, he argued was to be found in a restructuring of the educational system, with emphasis placed on teaching in the sciences. Loeb felt that the ability of individuals in the public eye, "men like [Theodore] Roosevelt and [Rudyard] Kipling" to sway public opinion would be severely curtailed. He was not hopeful about affecting the needed changes: "There is not much danger that such a state of education will come about in the next century, not if our present system of University administration continues."[33] As is evident Loeb, more than Dewey, became pessimistic, at times, that the educational system was capable of performing the task of "scientizing" students.

Certainly philosophers of science then and now could legitimately disagree with Loeb's unnecessarily narrow view of what constituted "science." Nowhere was this rigid interpretation more evident than in a letter Loeb wrote to the

---

32. Loeb to Joseph M. Park, 19 February 1915.

33. Loeb to A. G. Keller, 8 October 1915.

editor of *The Nation*.

> It might, however, be well to define what is meant by the term
> "our increasing knowledge of natural science, psychology, and
> anthropology." There is at present only one method known in
> science by which knowledge can increase, namely the method
> of quantitative experimentation, used generally by the physicist
> and chemist, used sparingly in natural science and psychology,
> and to the writer's knowledge not used at all in anthropology.
> Measured by this test, the theories of evolution cannot be
> considered an addition to our knowledge since they are not
> based upon experiments, though they have acted as a valuable
> stimulus in the revolt against church authority on the one
> hand, and on the other hand have furnished the excuse for the
> ruthlessness of imperialistic aggression. Measured by the test of
> the method of quantitative experimentation, "psycho-analysis"
> is no addition to our knowledge. Measured by the test of
> quantitative experimentation, the claims of "racial biologists,"
> teutonic and otherwise, are no addition to our knowledge,
> though they are playing an important role in the provocation
> of hatred and murder.[34]

Loeb's views on the nature of science, endorsing as they do only the
quantitative method, would clearly leave much of what passes for
scientific inquiry in the realm of pseudoscience at best, and probably
relegates much of the rest of it to disciplines which by definition can
never become scientific at all. However, in his own area(s) of
expertise he was convinced of the particular changes that should be
made to facilitate scientific training. He argued that physiology was
of necessity increasingly becoming the realm of chemistry and
physical chemistry; this reductionism was inevitable because, in the
final analysis, life phenomena were based on chemical and physical
processes. Because of this only a chemist or physical chemist could
adequately understand the processes of living matter, and only
someone so trained was equipped to teach the subject.[35]

However, Loeb did not believe that all his differences with other
scientists were because they were vitalists and he a mechanist. He was
well aware that many of his critics were simply unconvinced by his
experimental work. Loeb attributed this mostly to the fact that his
aim, among others, was to explain animal behavior through physical
chemistry by deriving the behavior quantitatively from such well–
established physical chemical effects as the Bunsen-Roscoe law. The

---

34. Loeb to Oswald Garrison Villard, 10 August 1918.

35. Loeb to Wilhelm Pfeffer, 24 August 1923.

latter was the principle in photochemistry that the effect of light on a photochemical compound (such as the emulsion on a photographic plate) is directly proportional to the product of time and light intensity; the same effect can be obtained with bright lights and short durations or dim lights and long durations ($I \times T = C$, with I as intensity, T as time and C as a constant), or any intervening appropriate combination of the two. Loeb argued that his experiments on the effect of light on organisms (heliotropisms) followed a similar mathematical relationship and provided strong support for the assertion that animal movements in response to light were simply the result of similar photochemical effects. He pointed out that his differences with the biologist Jennings (and others of his ilk) were not arguments of mechanism vs. vitalism, but were the result of Jennings's total ignorance of the physical chemistry that was the foundation of his own (Loeb's) experiments and conclusions. The vitalists, in turn, preferred the presentations of people like Jennings who did not bring physical chemistry into the discussion.[36]

At times Loeb seemed to believe that his own field of physiology was at a crossroads in terms of its development, for it was centuries behind that of physics. Loeb expressed strong admiration for the fields of physics, chemistry, and physical chemistry, and the progress made in those areas—they had become highly quantitative and mathematical in their methodology. Due to advances in the understanding of the particulate nature of compounds, molecules, and atoms the results of chemical reactions could be predicted with mathematical accuracy. As mentioned above, it was routine for the scientists to state the exact number of atoms of various elements that were in a given weight of a chemical compound. The development of the periodic table allowed those scientists to predict the existence and even specific atomic weight and nature of as yet undiscovered elements! Loeb repeatedly and emphatically pointed to the fields of physics, chemistry and physical chemistry as models to be emulated by physiology. The latter field, he felt, must wrench itself from its crude descriptive and speculative roots, which he considered almost prescientific, since he repeatedly expressed the conviction that physiology will emerge as a true science only when it is quantitative in measurement and mathematical in predictive formulation. As expressed in a letter to J. Pickering in 1923, "Biology, at present, is in about the same condition in which physics

---

36. Loeb to Richard Palmer, 25 May 1923. In this same letter Loeb also commented: "I cannot answer the question how the tropism theory can be applied to amoeba. Since by tropism theory I simply mean the determination of the direction of motion by physico-chemical forces, I have no doubt that in time this will be possible, but I have made no experiments on this form myself."

was in the 17th century. A few individuals are fighting hard to lay the foundation to a quantitative, and if possible to a mathematical, treatment of the subject, but they are voices crying in the wilderness." He feared that many individuals, scientists and non-scientists alike, saw the descriptive and taxonomic biology of the mid-nineteenth century as "the final form of that science."[37]

Loeb was especially critical of scientists within the field of biology as a whole. He felt that the potential advances of a physico-chemical, quantitative, mechanistic science of biology were being impeded in particular by "the ignorance and consequently the ill will of the profession—botanists, zoologists, and partly also physiologists."[38] Loeb's thoroughgoing mechanism and materialism thus made him skeptical not only of conservative religionists, but also of religious liberals because he thought that all too often their religiosity permeated their laboratory work and contaminated their scientific findings.

> I have not read Lillie's article in the *Scientific Monthly,* but I know him very well personally. He is by temperament a mystic and his wife, who has recently joined the Catholic Church and suffers from a religious hyper-emotionalism, influences him in the wrong direction. She is devoting her time to reading the life of the saints and makes everyone of her friends, whom she persuades, read that kind of stuff also. And since her husband's mind is given to nebulosity, I am afraid the result is showing in his work. . . . In the case of Conklin I do not know whether I wrote you that he started as a Methodist minister, and I think he is reverting to type. He has recently written a book which might have been written by a liberal minister, but which shows that he has not made any progress in scientific work. He is a charming fellow personally, as true a man as ever lived; but he has not had the training that enables him to leave the limits of descriptive morphology and he is unable to be critical in the field of experimental biology.[39]

Although Loeb's private correspondence often leaves his

---

37. Loeb to J. Pickering, 29 January 1923.

38. Loeb to Richard Palmer, 25 May 1923. "I think I still adhere to the views expressed in my book on *"The Organism as a Whole"* as far as heredity is concerned. The whole problem will one day be solved physico-chemically but physico-chemical biology is, as I hardly need to tell you, in its infancy and the worst hindrance of its development is the ignorance and consequently the ill will of the profession—botanists, zoologists, and partly also physiologists—towards the knowledge which has already been acquired." Loeb to J. Pickering, 29 January 1923.

39. Loeb to J. Pickering, 16 April 1921.

reader with the impression that he is waging a one-man battle on behalf of scientific materialism and secular humanism, the views he held were already shared by other intellectuals and members of the scientific community here and abroad. The British scientist J. Pickering was one such individual; in correspondence to Loeb, Pickering was scathing in his indictment of the negative effects of dualism on the condition of society. He felt that only with increased scientific knowledge of the mechanistic nature of the human body can the notion of soul, which he considered useless, be abandoned. He saw clerics and their ilk in a very negative light, being either stupid or self–serving. As he expressed it, they "are either persons with an undeveloped intellect or persons who are deliberately exploiting others in their own interests."[40]

Pickering, like Loeb, knew, however, that the problem lay not merely with the Christian Church and the clergy, but also with scientists and intellectuals who lent themselves to misguided or intellectually dishonest causes. Like Loeb he included some very eminent men in his indictments.

> It is, I suppose, one of the aftermaths of the recent outbreak of homicidal mania, that a great wave of supernaturalism and of superstition should be at present engulfing the majority of mankind. Partly is it to be accounted for by the extinction of all the best young minds of all the nations engaged in that insensate struggle. This wave of superstition shows itself in every walk of life. The pseudo philosopher of the stamp of [R. B.] Haldane publishes a book in which by some distortion of Einstein, he endeavors to re-instate a Hegelian system, which I had thought, was forever placed on a shelf. Men like his brother [J. B. S.] Haldane of Oxford, and Lodge of Birmingham use their position in the scientific world to advance these which they can have no possible knowledge of. The public knows their names as scientists, and unable to discriminate between the authority of a man in his specialty and his too often ignorance outside, concludes that the spiritism of Lodge and the vitalism of Haldane are facts of science. Were there only a wider dissemination of scientific truth among the public at large, they would be better able to judge of the value of a man's special work and the valuelessness of his speculations. It is this wider dissemination of scientific truth which appeals to me so strongly, and I am hoping that it will be possible to extend my lecturing so that the latest research of workers such as yourself, may be brought before an ever and rapidly increasing number of persons.[41]

---

40. J. Pickering to Loeb, 8 June 1921.

41. Ibid.

This, perhaps, explains why both Pickering and Loeb were willing to go on the lecture circuit to explain their point of view even at some expense and discomfort to themselves.

EPISTEMOLOGY

The reader of Loeb's correspondence with his friends and scientific colleagues cannot avoid the conclusion that he believed mechanistic materialism, the core of his social and scientific philosophy, would ultimately explain every vital aspect of human existence. However, as his life progressed, he gave up some of his earlier optimism that a mechanistic science would not only explain the human condition but also solve some of its many problems. In a letter to Pickering in 1921, he expressed the view that while he retained his belief in the potential of a mechanistic approach for solving social and political problems, he did not believe that it would soon be used to that end. He felt that a negative process of conditioning of the child was begun at infancy and continued to the point that the average citizen could be manipulated in a mob-like fashion through the use of simple phrases.[42] It is clear then that Loeb's epistemological stance was the basis for his larger view of the world; all paths ultimately lead back to mechanistic materialism.

The degree and the extent to which Loeb was willing to take the premises of mechanistic materialism and build a philosophy upon them was unusual, if not entirely novel, for an intellectual or scientist of his day. To illustrate, Charles Eliot, former president of Harvard University, had read an article by Loeb in the socialist *The New Review*. In this article Loeb had discussed topics such as human freedom and freedom of the will. Eliot wrote to Loeb seeking clarification of the meaning he assigned to these terms. In his reply, Loeb acknowledged that he had borrowed the concept of the degrees of freedom of human behavior from the field of physics wherein it is used to conceptualize the potential movements of various atoms and molecules. For instance, while a single atom has three degrees of freedom of movement along the axes of three dimensional space, a two-atom molecule, such as oxygen (O_2) has rotation capability around the common center of the two atoms for a total of five degrees of freedom. Loeb felt that human freedom of movement—"degrees of freedom"—was often restricted and constrained by social conditioning so that phrases such as "in

---

42. Loeb to J. Pickering, 14 February 1921.

defense of freedom" could compel action in a particular direction in an almost tropismatic manner.[43]

That Loeb was contemptuous of religionists who tried to mix science and religion is beyond doubt. What is perhaps unusual about his opposition to the confusion between the two realms is his continuing effort to set the record straight and undermine those he believed were behaving in an unscientific manner.

> What you write to me about Storm van Leuwen was very amusing but not surprising. The man was formerly a cavalry officer and I think he is also a devout Catholic. Moreover, he is a product of Prof. Magnus in Utrecht, who is a vitalist and a friend of von Uexküll who writes biology in the style of Houston Chamberlain to whom he dedicated one book and another he dedicated to Count Eulenburg, the famous chief of the Round Table who had some unpleasant experiences in court. I suppose this will help you to understand his remarks to you. The sad part is that such idiots ever get positions in universities.[44]

Yet, measured by his own standards, Loeb was not an unreasonable critic of the work of others. Indeed, he sometimes praised scientific contributions by individuals with whose extra-scientific ideas he could not possibly have agreed. In a letter to the Scottish scientist and author John Authur Thomson (1861-1933), Loeb expressed both praise of a scientist with whom he often disagreed and a scathing indictment of a philosopher whose ideas he regarded as pernicious. Loeb felt that while he disagreed with Thomson and Hans Driesch on the interpretation of certain scientific results, such disagreements only stimulated further productive dialogue and disputation, essential ingredients of the scientific process. However, in the same letter, Loeb expressed in the strongest possible language his disagreement with Thomson's high regard for the French philosopher Bergson, for whom, as we have seen, he had nothing but contempt.[45]

Some of Loeb's efforts to undermine religious belief, especially the more ignorant kinds of fundamentalism, exhibit considerable pragmatism and prudence on his part. For example, a school teacher, George C. Taylor, who lived in Albuquerque, New Mexico, wrote to him to complain that he was constantly in trouble with his superintendent and the parents of his students because of his views

43. Loeb to Charles Eliot, 10 February 1915.

44. Loeb to P. H. DeKruif, 26 June 1923.

45. Loeb to John Arthur Thomson, 26 January 1917.

on evolution. Taylor also mentioned that a recent traveling evangelist had authoritatively stated that most prominent leaders in science had abandoned the theory of evolution and that his own, Taylor's, outspoken disagreement had only resulted in "a good deal of ridicule upon my innocent head." He requested that Loeb reply with comments on the subject.[46]

In one of his replies to Taylor, Loeb's realism was clearly evident. Though he wanted to help Taylor, he did not want him to become entangled in a situation that might cost him his job, nor did he want Taylor involved in controversy that exceeded his grasp of evolutionary theory. Loeb forwarded some newspaper articles which he felt might support Taylor's position. However, he said, one of the articles was for Taylor's own edification and was not to be circulated—it being "too aggressive." While assuring Taylor that evolutionary theory remained in good scientific standing, he cautioned the teacher not to risk his own position as it would "hurt you personally and do the cause no good."[47]

Loeb's keen interest in keeping abreast of developments in his own field and helping others do the same was nowhere better exemplified than in an exchange between himself and B. K. Kingsbury, who held an appointment in the Department of Histology and Embryology at the Cornell University Medical College. In a letter to Loeb, Kingsbury passed along a request from a colleague for information on the philosophical aspects of the concept of "function." The originator of this request was E. B. Titchener, an eminent professor of psychology at Cornell and the founder of the laboratory of experimental psychology at that university.[48]

Loeb's answer to Kingsbury and Titchener was revealing because he not only engaged in some ideological ax-grinding of his own, but provided them with the updated information they requested. Loeb declared that the term "function," along with the terms "stimulus" and "stimulation" had been dropped from use in the field of physiology. He further asserted that they had come into use in the first place "out of sheer embarrassment, owing to the fact that they ["earlier physiologists"] did not fully realize the purely chemical basis of life phenomena." Loeb absolved these "earlier physiologists" of guilt in the matter since physical chemistry did not exist at the time the now unnecessary terms were incorporated into physiology. Loeb stated that in the modern science of biology the

46. George C. Taylor to Loeb, 14 April 1913.

47. Loeb to George C. Taylor, 7 May 1913.

48. B. F. Kingsbury to Loeb, 30 November 1918.

terms had "been found useless." After further expressions of support for the modern "physico-chemical" mechanistic study of the life processes, Loeb referred Dr. Titchener to two of his (Loeb's) books *The Organism as a Whole* and *Forced Movements, Tropisms, and Animal Conduct* "where he can see the treatment of such a subject as this without these terms."[49]

Loeb was dismayed at times by what he regarded as the backward metaphysical and religious views of the scientific community. For example, on 9 July 1917 he wrote to his friend in Stockholm, the Swedish physical chemist Svante Arrhenius that:

> I have been very grateful to you for your kind words about my book. Lillie, who reviewed it in the *Journal of the American Chemical Society*, is a good deal of a mystic, as are the majority of zoologists; they do not realize that all life phenomena are determined by rigid laws and that these laws can have a mathematical expression. Thus my theory of tropisms is vigorously antagonized by mystic anthropomorphic hypotheses of the zoologists and, on the whole even men like Professor Wilson of Columbia University do not think very highly of a physico-chemical explanation of life phenomena.[50]

Loeb was also negative in his judgments of the social intelligence of other scientists for he told Arrhenius in the same letter that "even physicists—men like Hale or Michelson—when they leave the field of physics and deal with human affairs from an anthropomorphic viewpoint . . . the result is all kinds of fanaticism."[51] Or as Loeb put it in another context, the objective of modern biology was no longer the mere understanding, but also the control of life-phenomena, a view which he linked with moral and social ideals which, at his death in 1924, still sought a vehicle for their political realization.

---

49. Loeb to B. F. Kingsbury, 3 December 1918.

50. Loeb to Svante Arrhenius, 9 July 1917.

51. Ibid.

CHAPTER THREE
JACQUES LOEB
AND THE GREAT WAR

———◆———

Although Loeb displayed interest in many domestic and international political events, nothing so engrossed his attention and that of his American wife as the events surrounding the First World War. The War directly affected Loeb's immediate family, his European friends and relatives in Germany and Austria, in the countries the Central Powers occupied, and in the neutral countries near their borders. Many of his letters contain commentary on the nature of the War itself, its effects on the Western scientific community, and its political and economic ramifications throughout the world.

Loeb possessed a strong streak of pacifism. It appears, however, that his pacifist tendencies were tempered by political realism. To make matters more complex, even though Loeb detested the Hohenzollern regime and its military machine, he was otherwise a germanophile, that is, a lover of German culture. This affected his attitudes toward Germany's wartime enemies especially England, for although he had English friends of scientific eminence including physicist Ernest Rutherford and biologist Julian Huxley, he was no anglophile. At times, he was almost as willing to attribute the War to Britain as to Germany and, in any case, he disliked what he perceived as British insularity and snobbishness.

Our story of Loeb and the Great War begins shortly after the German march into Belgium in August, 1914. On 23 October 1914 Loeb wrote to the Swedish physical chemist, his friend and confidante in Stockholm, Svante Arrhenius. Loeb professed amusement that both he and Arrhenius were being "bombarded" by both British and German fellow scientists, each claiming that his nation was taking the noble path in their respective prosecution of the war. But Loeb soon singled out the German "emperor and his military caste . . . for the . . . incredible piece of barbarism" in their treatment of the Belgian people. He goes on to decry any military organization and bemoans having to be "confronted every day with these deeds of barbarity."[1]

Loeb's pacifist tendencies are pronounced at this point in the War as he blames all sides for the debacle. However, later in the letter despite his germanophilic tendencies, he was able to detect certain flaws in German culture which were less in evidence in the Allied nations. Loeb observed that Americans were generally outraged at German violation of Belgian neutrality and at German abuse of and demands for war support from the Belgian people. He concludes that, as a result of resentment of German conduct in Belgium, Americans almost unanimously oppose Germany and there is in the letter a subtle suggestion that he, Loeb, concurs. Loeb labels the German attitude of racial superiority a "conceit" and a "form of insanity." He attributes a major role in the outbreak of the war to misguided notions of race and morality. He concludes that the "Slavs believe their race is the chosen one and the Germans believe that the Teutonic race represents the superman."[2]

Loeb believed at the outset of the War that its immediate cause was the aggressive behavior of the Central Powers. He declared as much in an October, 1914 letter to friend and fellow scientist Wilhelm Ostwald in Leipzig. While he expressed relief that thus far the war was outside the boundaries of Germany and hoped it would remain so, he made it clear that Americans supported the French and Belgians. While he claimed in the letter to be describing American popular opinion, he also seemed to be describing his own when he stated that the hostile move of the Central Powers, Austria in particular, into Serbia was completely unjustified and should have been referred to the World Court at the Hague.[3]

Loeb thus indicated his preference for settling differences among nations through internationally recognized conflict resolution mechanisms. He also criticized Emperor Wilhelm II for glorifying the German army "on every suitable and unsuitable occasion." In the same 1914 letter to Ostwald, Loeb commented that it was his perception that Americans held a strong antipathy toward the military caste system in Germany and have a desire to see the system disappear with the conclusion of the war which, they are convinced, Germany will eventually lose. Interestingly, Loeb also expressed his own strong opinion to the contrary,

1. Loeb to Svante Arrhenius, 23 October 1914.

2. Ibid.

3. Loeb to Wilhelm Ostwald, 10 October 1914.

stating that Germany would eventually win the war. He also observed that, in spite of their distaste for the German military, "Americans sympathize with the German scientists and the German people."[4]

Although in the early stages of the War Loeb thought Germany would emerge victorious, he was later to change his mind especially after the entry of the United States on the side of the Allies in April, 1917. Nevertheless, his deep humanistic and pacifist bent made him skeptical of the moralistic claims articulated by both sides. In December 1914, he wrote to the American socialist William English Walling that:

> There is no question that Germans and Russians alike are guided by purely chauvinistic principles. When war began, it was stated that the English and their Allies were going to protect the rights of the small nationalities. It was greeted with approval in England, when the Russian Commander in Chief announced to the Poles that the Russians had come to liberate them and that an autonomous Poland was to be founded. At the same time, the Czar issued a friendly manifesto to his beloved Jews. The Germans, not to stand behind, issued similar declarations. Now the war rages in Poland. The Jews are denounced by both sides as spies and are murdered on short notice. . . . One does not know any more on what side to stand. The whole war is against liberty and humanity, and the after-effects will last for decennials if not a great social revolution comes.[5]

As the war continued, Loeb became even more skeptical of the motivations of all sides including nonparticipants such as the United States. Perhaps more importantly, he began to look for structural causes of war and militarism and found them in the armaments industry. He was ever suspicious that the motives and actions of the same group, the munitions makers, might eventually bring this country into the quagmire of the European war. In another letter to Wilhelm Ostwald, this one dated July 1915, Loeb observed that in America, "Our capitalistic papers, like the New York Times . . . ." work to justify a continuation of the war and consider such circumstances as might necessitate American entry into the conflict. Loeb pointed to such sloganeering as "our dignity is at stake" and to the fact that similar strident statements in European papers had preceded the

---

4. Ibid.

5. Loeb to William English Walling, 21 December 1914.

original outbreak of war on the continent. In this letter he
repeatedly named Roosevelt as one of the "political adventurers..."
who "preached militarism," and, along with "... the naval and
army castes..." will eventually "... manage to run us into a war
or at least an armed camp." Because of the huge profits made
from the manufacture of armaments, Loeb saw an almost
irresistible wave of militaristic sentiment in the United States
which would, he feared, continue well after the war's end. "It has
never been so clearly demonstrated that wars are made for profits
as it is in America just now" he concluded. Once again, Loeb did
not spare the English, whom he saw as perfectly willing and even
eager to continue the war as their own ends are served and "the
French, Italians, Russians, and other dupes are willing to pull
the chestnuts out of the fire for them." Loeb added, "When all
the rest are ruined, the English will have an easy time of it." With
apparent pessimism he observed that in America there was no
longer a focus on the means by which to bring about peace and
the means of maintaining peace once it was achieved. The focus
of attention was on war.[6]

At this point in the War, Loeb's humanism and pacifism
seemed to give way at least temporarily to a despairing cynicism as
he articulated sentiments that might have come from a
practitioner of realpolitik. A few months later, he wrote again to
the Swedish physical chemist Svante Arrhenius in even more
cynical tones, "The war still goes on merrily; as Bernard Shaw put
it 'they wanted a belly full of fight' and I think they are getting it."
Loeb saw that the United States was in the grip of a pervasive war
propaganda, leading to ever–increasing militaristic sentiments;
and all of this, he felt, was driven by the enormous profits
accruing from the sale of armaments to the combatants. The
major bankers (he named J. P. Morgan specifically) arranged the
contracts between the Allied governments and the producers in
America. For this they earned a profit. He surmised that the same
banker received a kickback from the company receiving the
contract—another profit. The same banker, Loeb continues,
bought the producer's stock prior to the announcement of the
contract, and sold some after the announcement—another profit.
So as long as the war continues, Loeb observed, these bankers
continue to reap ever–increasing sums of money. In the
meantime, he argued, the country's financial markets are awash
in stock whose value is maintained only so long as the war profits
continue; thus, to profiteering is added, in Loeb's eyes, the real

---

6. Loeb to Wilhelm Ostwald, 31 July 1915.

risk of an economic collapse.[7]

As the War wore on and it became apparent that the United States would soon become involved, Loeb, who had two sons of draft age, became concerned: On 9 February 1917 he wrote to his eldest son Leonard to this effect.

> I am afraid that war is only a question of a few days and for that reason I want to write to you giving you my viewpoint of how you should act. I suppose we both agree that war is about the most brutal and stupid of all things and that the military regime is less intelligent than any other regime, except perhaps the theologians'. For that reason I think you should realize that your service as a scientist is of more value to the country than your value as cannon fodder; and I think the case of Hostley has sufficiently shown that. In Germany and England the young scientists are no longer sent to the front. For this reason I want you to keep out of any enlistment in any patriotic way without consulting with me, and if anybody should talk to you, you can tell them that there is an agreement between you and me that you should not act except upon consultation with me.[8]

Although Loeb probably believed by this point in the War that an Allied victory over the Central Powers was the lesser of two evils, he still apparently favored a neutral course for America. In the same letter to his son, Loeb argued that in spite of the intolerable militaristic behavior of Germany, President Wilson could have

---

7. Loeb to Svante Arrhenius, 7 October 1915.

 I have not written to you for a long time because the ferocious character the war in Europe has assumed recently has depressed me too much. I had hoped that spring might see the end of the war but it becomes more and more apparent to me that England is really determined to crush Germany completely, at the expense of France, Russia, and anybody else they can induce to fight their battles. The English are surely not better than the Germans, but they are much more hypocritical. I think they have now cast off the last attempt of posing for the sake of humanity; now it is nothing but a destruction of German commerce. I do not think the German nor the English will learn the lesson that to go around armed and to aspire to an empire of the world does not lead to anything decent. Here in America the press continues to be on the side of the English, chiefly because the Allies have given enormous orders for ammunition and so bring business to the country. It becomes brutally obvious that business runs the world.

Loeb to Arrhenius, 24 February 1915.

 I think the one country which is the most violently opposed to peace is America, because it prospers too much on the sins of war, and President Wilson would make himself very unpopular with the manufacturers and the big bankers if he began to work for peace now.

Ibid.

8. Jacques Loeb to Leonard Loeb, 18 February 1917.

remained neutral, curtailed relations with both sides in the conflict, and thus allowed America to avoid all involvement in the war.[9]

Loeb's attitudes toward the possible conscription of his sons was evident in his general view of armies and the military life. He had no illusions regarding the nature of militarism in any form or country, perhaps stemming from his own experience with the Imperial German Army before he emigrated. In a 1917 letter written to Amos Pinchot, Loeb argued that the rich and the powerful will inevitably control any army. Citing Switzerland as an example where it was "practically only the sons of the patricians who were filling the positions of officers," Loeb argued that even where an attempt was made to achieve a democratic army the result was a "hollow mockery." He pointed out that "in Switzerland in order to avoid this danger, they passed a law giving the officer the money for his uniform, but even that did not help." He argued that "a 'democratic army' has thus far never existed," and that Americans should understand that in this country such an army is even less likely since "Wall street and its henchmen are sure to command any army that the United States may organize." He concluded after that statement, "I think no political prediction could be more safely made than this one."[10]

Apparently, Loeb's son Leonard, who had a doctorate in physics and held a civilian post in the government in Washington, cherished pacifist sentiments of a sort and was strongly opposed to American entry into the War. On 30 March 1917, just three weeks prior to the U.S. declaration of war, Loeb sent the following advice to his son:

> If the war hysteria should break out in the Bureau please tell those who might bother you that you promised me not to enlist for any kind of service without first consulting with me. It is now fashionable here to imitate the English and the French in trying to get people to enlist though there is no necessity for that amount of enlistment which they ask for. Do not allow politicians and the money lenders of Wall Street to exploit you for their selfish ends. On the other hand, I should not express

---

9. Ibid.

10. Loeb to Amos Pinchot, 28 February 1917. Earlier, on 20 February 1917 he told Pinchot that:
> I have been very much depressed over the recent developments in this country. I left Germany because I felt that I could not live in a regime of oppression such as Bismarck had created at the time I left Europe [1891].
> When I reached America I felt like a free being with a load off my shoulders.
On 30 March 1917 he informed Pinchot that he and a colleague had communicated directly to President Wilson their support for continued avoidance of American involvement in the European war.

any violent anti-war sentiments. The majority of the people are too hysterical and one has to be as careful with them in one's utterance as with people who are dangerously insane. The only thing to do is to stick more thoroughly to your work, and engross yourself more deeply in scientific problems in order to keep your minds and forget the insanity around you.[11]

Clearly, Loeb was politically sensitive and sufficiently realistic about public opinion to recognize that his son would have an easier time of it if he avoided being outspoken on the war issue.

As soon as the U.S. entered the War, Loeb began to abandon his expressions of neutrality. Surprisingly, on 28 May 1917 he wrote to his son Leonard expressing a high regard for President Wilson's idealism. He felt that the President had "tried in every way to avoid the war" and that, in the final analysis, American entry into the war at the present time was probably necessary in order to avoid going to war at some future time, "under more unfavorable conditions." Even more surprising, Loeb argued that given its arguments of the necessity of entering the conflict "the government should have the benefit of the doubt." He continues, "The beastly brutality of the Germans in not heeding Wilson's demands of dropping that ruthless submarine warfare forced Wilson's hand." In the same letter to his son, Loeb expresses considerable support for the purchase of Liberty Bonds, ". . . under the circumstances, I think the least an employee of the government can do—and in my opinion every citizen—is to buy a bond." He adds, "I myself have bought ten bonds."[12] It appears that temporarily, at least, Loeb put aside his dislike of American militarism, suspended judgment on the role of Wall Street and war profiteers in promoting war, and backed the Allied cause. German submarine warfare and German brutality in the occupied countries may have convinced him that neutrality even for an intellectual and scientist like himself was no longer a viable option. On the other hand it is possible that Loeb's expressions of support of the American cause and the justness of President Wilson's position were a result of his audience; he was writing this letter to a son who might very well be a party to the

---

11. Jacques Loeb to Leonard Loeb, 30 March 1917.

12. Ibid., 28 May 1917. Later in 1917, Loeb told Julian Huxley that:
    Wilson is probably both right and sincere in his statement that the world cannot remain half democratic and half autocratic. It would be very important that the German people should be told that it is seriously the opinion of the democratic peoples themselves and not only of their governments that the rule of the German and Austrian Princelings should come to an end and that at least Germany should be given a democratic constitution.
    Loeb to Huxley, 20 August 1917.

conflict one day soon. Loeb may have felt it was in his son's interests if he, the father, expressed support for the country's new direction.

A few weeks later, however, in a letter to the noted Dutch biologist Hugo de Vries, the father of mutation theory, he reverted to his old opinions and commentary concerning the war. He complained of a "state of depression" arising from American entry into the war; he fervently wished that "we may see peace soon." He reiterated his belief that the war was being maintained because of the profits pouring into the hands of powerful and influential businessmen and bankers; he saw other war aims as being to gain control of trade with Russia and South America. The only positive outcome of the war thus far, as he saw it, was the transformation of Russia into a republic; he said that if Germany also were to become a republic "then the nightmare of a repetition of such slaughter may be avoided."[13]

LOEB, CREEL AND THE COMMITTEE ON PUBLIC INFORMATION

When the United States entered the War, George Creel was appointed chairman of the Committee on Public Information which was a federal agency charged with the creation of a favorable environment through publicity on behalf of the prosecution of American war aims. The Committee, which also included the Secretaries of State, War and Navy, asked Loeb to participate in an organization whose ostensible objective was to foment the martial spirit. Their interest in Loeb was, no doubt, due in part to his eminence as a scientist; but it was also due to the Committee's perception of him as a German-American. On 27 October 1917, Creel wrote Loeb a letter introducing a Mr. J. Koettgen, Organizing Secretary of the Friends of German Democracy. In this letter to Loeb, Creel endorsed Koettgen's "ability, sincerity and motives" and went on to support the formation of German-American organizations in every state, whose apparent purpose would be to demonstrate that it is ultimately in the interests of "the fatherland" for loyal German-Americans to support this country's aims and goals in the great European conflict.[14]

Loeb's reply was an interesting one because it showed considerable political acumen on his part. On 4 December 1917 he

13. Loeb to Hugo de Vries, 26 June 1917.

14. George Creel to Loeb, 27 October 1917.

told Creel that:

> Mr. Koettgen brought me your letter of introduction and I am
> in hearty sympathy with parts of his plan. I think the Germans
> in Switzerland, working for an overthrow of their government,
> should be supported with all the means at your disposal;
> moreover, I think it would be very important to spread
> revolutionary literature among German prisoners not only in
> France but also in England. In order to overcome the possible
> influence of their officers, I think it might be a good scheme to
> separate the men from their officers, and, furthermore, to
> organize the men in the prison camps in England so that
> German Socialists and revolutionary Germans are in charge of
> each group of them, otherwise the officers and loyalists among
> the Germans will oppose all efforts at democratization. I think
> Mr. Koettgen is the right man to select the proper literature.[15]

Loeb knew enough about the officer corps in the German army to
recognize that it was unlikely to hold much democratic sentiment;
he was also shrewd to suspect that not all opponents of German
militarism were necessarily in favor of constitutional democracy. In
what may be a cryptic reference to the presence of radical political
extremists among the rank-and-file he wrote:

> It is barely possible that those Germans who would join a
> movement directed against German militarism and against the
> German government are of a somewhat different type, but I
> have no guarantee.[16]

However, Loeb's main problem in this letter was not the accurate
forecasting or analysis of political change; rather, it was to explain as
politely as possible to Creel why he did not wish to join the
organization. He stated, using diplomatic language, that he had left
Germany twenty-six years earlier and had avoided German
associations entirely during that time because of "the aggressive
insolence and brutality . . . of many Germans [due to] the influence
of militarism." This long separation from things German, in

---

15. Loeb to George Creel, 4 December 1917. "As far as the foundation of a society
in this country for an overthrow of the present German government is
concerned, Mr. Koettgen thinks that most Germans would be scared at the idea
of a German republic, while I believe that there is no reason to be afraid of
impressing such an idea. I am afraid, however, that the grip of German feudalism
is too tight to expect the possibility of a republic in the near future; but the
expression of the idea will act as a ferment for the future and can do no harm."
Ibid.

16. Ibid.

combination with his American wife, American children and American friends resulted in his having little in common with German-Americans—or so he claimed. He thus declined the invitation, but endorsed the selection of Koettgen to lead the effort.[17]

Given Loeb's pacifist tendencies, it is easy to understand why he would not want to join any organizations that might be used for propagandistic war purposes or be subjected to government manipulation in pursuit of its military and diplomatic aims. Nevertheless, it is also evident that Loeb was politically shrewd to realize that he had little to gain from alienating Creel or his powerful agency.

BOLSHEVISM AND LOEB'S REACTION

Like many American intellectuals, Loeb was most pleased with the collapse of the Romanoff Dynasty in February 1917. Indeed, on the eve of American entry into the War, Loeb commented in a letter to the American socialist William English Walling that his "feelings about the entry of this country into the war are divided, but I think Wilson's statement was in many ways excellent especially his endorsement of the Russian revolution."[18] Loeb was, of course, referring to the fall of the Czarist regime during the February Revolution that brought the Provisional Government and Alexander Kerensky to power, not to the Bolshevik coup which occurred later in October 1917. In the aftermath of the Bolshevik Revolution, Loeb wrote revealingly of his attitudes toward Communism in a letter to his friend Arrhenius; he considered Communism to be the "worst danger." While he did not feel that Communists goals were within their abilities to achieve them, he feared that in making the attempt, they might "succeed in upsetting civilization pretty thoroughly." In this same letter, he comments on the war in general, blaming the German capitalists in concert with German militarists for starting the war. He expresses concern over postwar militarism in America and the fact that the war's end, "has fostered the revolutionary spirit among the workingmen who are now demanding things which are incompatible with the continuation of our civilization." In general he saw the war as producing many social changes, few of which he regarded as beneficial.[19]

---

17. Ibid.

18. Loeb to William English Walling, 3 April 1917.

19. Loeb to Svante Arrhenius, 23 January 1919.

Loeb was politically astute enough to recognize how political extremism of the Left and Right were linked together, the one giving rise to the other. The spread of Bolshevism in Germany at the end of the War encouraged extremism of the Right and the brutal murder of Karl Liebnecht and Rosa Luxembourg was, in turn, followed by the rightist Kapp Putsch and Hitler's premature effort to seize power in Bavaria. Loeb watched the volatile and unstable situation with a careful eye as political extremists on both sides jockeyed with each other for power and in a letter to a German acquaintance commented that:

> The conditions in Europe are gone from bad to worse and I only hope that Germany will be spared the experience of a "white terror." I am not an admirer of Freud, but if the history of Germany since Bismarck is written, it can be put under the one heading of a nation acting like a brutal megalomaniac on account of an inferiority complex.[20]

Although Loeb was a man of the Left, he opposed political extremists of any kind. This may have been a consequence of the fact that he considered himself a product of the Age of Reason and liked to recite its litany, or it might have been his strong pacifist tendencies which caused him to dislike the use of force and violence. Whatever the case, he does not appear to have liked Bolshevism, once he realized its nature, any better than he liked the proto-fascist movements of the early 1920s which were already rearing their ugly heads.

As the War continued, Loeb became ever more appalled by the carnage especially after his son Leonard went to France. As the final German offensive of the War on the Western front ground to a halt, Loeb wrote to his former student, biochemist Thorburn Brailsford Robertson in Berkeley in April 1918 expressing hope that the offensive would end soon, but also expressing fear that "the Germans will keep up their carnival of murder." He was obviously concerned over the lack of news from his son Leonard, last known to be in Paris.[21]

Interestingly, Loeb had already begun to anticipate the nature of the peace agreement that might follow the cessation of hostilities. On January 31, 1918 Loeb told his son Leonard that labor unrest in Germany might hasten the end of the war; this, combined with the Russian Revolution, labor unrest in Britain and labor's general

---

20. Loeb to Otto Meyerhof, 15 November 1923.

21. Loeb to T. B. Robertson, 2 April 1918.

demand for participation in a peace conference made Loeb hopeful about a "decent peace."[22]

ANGLOPHOBIA

Unlike many American academics of his time Loeb was not an anglophile. Indeed, his correspondence during World War I indicates a distrust of the British government, a dislike of several of its policies, and an indifferent attitude toward various aspects of English life and culture. In a 1915 letter to his friend Arrhenius, Loeb expressed his rather low regard for British motives in pursuing the war with such tenacity; the force that drives them, he asserted, is "business," not love of freedom or the ideal of independence for small nations. He felt that British treatment of Greece was of the same order as that of the Germans toward the Belgians. In fact, he stated in the letter that "I almost begin to believe that the Germans are right in stating that if they had not marched into Belgium first the French and English would surely have done so."[23]

Earlier that year he had commented to Arrhenius that "I feel that the English are not much better than the Germans but that they are only much shrewder."[24] However, the bulk of his criticism of Britain focused primarily on the alleged egoism and the condescending, patronizing attitudes of English scientists in their dealings with scientific colleagues around the world. He remained critical of British military and diplomatic policy, yet it was the perceived elitist attitudes of British science that disturbed him the most. Loeb's resentment seemed to stem in part from the bad effects English scientific snobbery allegedly had on young American scientists: On 16 November 1923 he wrote to W. J. V. Osterhout that:

> I expect when Fenn comes back now, he will find difficulty in getting through the door of any American laboratory. [A. R.] Moore told me that when he met him last fall in England, he had already an outrageously swelled head, a phenomenon of growth which is to be anticipated in the case of any young American who goes to England to work. I suppose the

22. Jacques Loeb to Leonard Loeb, 13 January 1918.

23. Loeb to Svante Arrhenius, 7 October 1915.

24. Ibid., 8 May 1915.

mechanism is that they tell him that all scientists in America are rotten and that he, the young man, is the only exception, having had sense enough to make a pilgrimage to the true shrine of science.[25]

Months after the war was over Loeb complained bitterly that the English continued to censor all mail coming from the continent to America, causing a considerable delay in communications. "I wonder whether for the rest of our lives the English censor will open all our letters," he exclaimed. Loeb was particularly incensed that American scientists had not received any professional publications from the Central Powers "since 1915, while the English get everything. It is beyond my comprehension why we should be forbidden to read scientific papers printed in the German language." Loeb suggested a paternalism on the part of the English in deciding what scientific material should be read by Americans. He exclaimed, "I think of all the peculiarities of the war, the continuation of this intellectual guardianship of England over the United States is the most amusing." Loeb's claims to the contrary notwithstanding, it is difficult for the reader to discern any humorous intent in these comments to Arrhenius.[26]

Again in March 1919 in another letter to Osterhout he complained of English attitudes of superiority; in their view, as Loeb saw, scientific work conducted outside of Britain was inherently inferior, to be taken lightly, and to be measured against the superior standard of English excellence. He referred to the "bullying methods of English scientists" whom he felt viewed Americans "as their vassals."[27]

LOEB ON PACIFISM AND PATRIOTISM

In his correspondence and perhaps also in his conversations with friends and colleagues, Loeb often referred to himself as a "pacifist." Our intent here is to discuss what Loeb meant by this and just how principled he was in applying what to him were fundamental moral and political principles to matters of peace and war.

"Pacifism" is usually taken to mean moral aversion to the use of force to resolve disputes whether between individuals or nations.

25. Loeb to W. J. V. Osterhout, 16 November 1923.

26. Loeb to Svante Arrhenius, 4 February 1919.

27. Loeb to W. J. V. Osterhout, 13 March 1919.

With Loeb, it seems to have meant mostly the latter since he apparently did not oppose the use of coercion against criminals or others who used violent means to get their way. His pacifism, then, was focused primarily on international conflict to which he was highly averse. Nevertheless, his pacifism was of a qualified kind even here and his application of it was sometimes inconsistent, but even his inconsistency is instructive from the point of view of understanding the role of the scientist in politics. Ironically, Loeb was often intellectually and verbally aggressive in asserting his pacifism, as inconsistent as this may seem. Probably what prevented him from being even more assertive was his belief that domestic political policy and international affairs lay outside his realm of expertise. As he put it:

> Naturally I am an antimilitarist, but when it comes to public expression I may go as far as signing a petition of a number of people against militarism, but I do not see what claim I have to stand out [as] a spokesman for antimilitarists. Sargent can do so with full propriety;—so can any practicing physician—but I, who [have] never practiced medicine, could only go to a hearing intended for practicing physicians under false pretenses, and I must not do that. When I gave my talk on Biology and War I carefully selected these topics where I felt I could speak with expert knowledge, and where I could tell things in mind [when] those with less knowledge and biological experience could not speak as efficiently.[28]

Loeb's professional conscience as a scientist thus made it impossible for him to pretend competence to speak against policies that he found immoral when he lacked the standing to do so, but again his behavior was not fully consistent. Loeb's pacifism could not always stand scrutiny on other grounds either. A letter he wrote to a French scientific friend whose son had just been killed in action provides evidence of this. Following his expressions of sympathy, Loeb suggested that since the war could be considered "a continuation of the French Revolution . . . pacifists can participate in it and sacrifice the best and dearest we have." On one hand, these phrases raise a number of questions concerning the nature of Loeb's pacifism. On the other hand, the letter may be one of compassion for an individual who has recently suffered a terrible blow, the loss of a son, rather than an accurate expression of Loeb's views on war and violence.[29]

28. Loeb to Dr. James P. Warbasse, 18 January 1917.

29. Loeb to Charles Richet, 25 October 1918.

It is also important to note that this letter was written *after* the United States, Loeb's adopted country, entered the War and *after* Loeb's two sons went into the U.S. Army. His correspondence during this period indicates this had a considerable impact in helping him rationalize his own support for the Allied cause. Loeb even lost sight of his own equivocation regarding war and American participation in it, to the point of buying U.S. war bonds and urging others to do so.

While Loeb apparently continued to regard himself as a principled "pacifist," it is evident that this was a misnomer if taken literally as a description of his behavior. Clearly, he had a strong animus against militarism; yet apparently he did not oppose the use of force when there was no alternative to stopping the German war machine.[30] However, a letter Loeb wrote early in the War may hold the key to understanding the enigma of his pacifism or at least clarify its meaning:

> Your suggestion that this country assume the leadership in a league of neutral nations rather than go to war meets with my heartiest approval. It is hardly necessary to state that nobody has anything to gain in a war except the armament mongers, the war contractors, the army and navy castes, and certain political adventurers. It should not be overlooked that in addition to the suffering which any war causes, a war with Germany would bring endless anguish to all those Americans who were born in Germany or who are descendants of Germans. *There is only one case in which war might be defensible and that is when a country is actually in danger of invasion by a hostile army; but this danger does not exist for us.*[31] [author's emphasis]

A principled pacifist would not hold this position since it sanctions the use of force to repel invaders. Loeb's statement here leads to serious reservations about whether he really understood the meaning of "pacifism"—a term which he often used. Loeb probably would have been well advised simply to distinguish between "just" and "unjust" wars rather than to claim himself a principled "pacifist." When he referred to himself and other like-minded individuals as "neutrals," he was closer to his real position on the European war than when he invoked the term "pacifist."

Nevertheless, it is well to keep in mind, as Mulford Sibley argues, that "pacifism" has possessed both a broad and a narrow

---

30. Loeb to Wolfgang Pauli, 28 June 1920.

31. Loeb to L. Hollingsworth Wood, 10 May 1915.

meaning.[32] In the broad sense, it was often employed in the earlier part of this century to indicate those outlooks which focus on the need for peacemaking and international reconciliation machinery. In this usage many intellectual tendencies could be labeled "pacifist" since the word was used to describe a wide spectrum of activities and ideas that might potentially be peacemaking in nature. From this perspective, two of Loeb's contemporaries, Jean Jaures, the French socialist leader, and Woodrow Wilson were both pacifists and organizations like the Carnegie Endowment for International Peace were pacifistic.[33]

More recently, however, pacifism has come to mean those ideas and movements that repudiate the use of violence, especially war, under any and all circumstances. This kind of pacifist believes that war, whether aggressive or defensive, is always morally illegitimate and, in the long run, ineffective for the achievement of desired goals.[34]

Loeb, in writing and theorizing about "pacifism," tended to use both the broad and the narrow definitions and since he did this inconsistently, it is often difficult to tell precisely what he means. He was unable to make up his mind, except for short periods, whether to repudiate the use of physical force altogether, at least as a means of resolving conflict between nations, or endorse it to repel invaders in the case of unprovoked aggression.[35]

Like his friend and former colleague Thorstein Veblen, who wrote so tellingly of patriotism in *The Nature of Peace*, Loeb mostly saw the negative aspects of the term. That is to say, he saw how patriotism was used by vested interests to manipulate the common man into supporting policies that were contrary to his best interests. Perhaps as a European émigré of Jewish background it was easier for Loeb to detect the ways in which patriotism was used to justify immoral policies and to discredit those opposed to the machinations of the vested interests. In a 1916 letter to the socialist Max Eastman, Loeb recalled the misuse of patriotism in both Germany and Russia; in the former, expressions of support for the actions and policies of Bismarck were considered laudable and comments in opposition to those actions and policies were thought unpatriotic while in the latter case, "it would be considered extremely unpatriotic to suggest that the Romanoffs be

---

32. Mulford Sibley, "Pacifism," *International Encyclopedia of the Social Sciences,* David Sills, edit. Vol. II (New York: Macmillan Company and Free Press, 1968) pp. 353-57.

33. Ibid.

34. Ibid.

35. Ibid.

retired to private life." Loeb continued by pointing out that in America any expression of dissent from the established policy of selling munitions to certain combatants in the European conflict was considered "extremely unpatriotic." He provided other examples of allegedly "unpatriotic" expressions of opinion such as arguments that arms manufacturing should be the sole preserve of the United States government in order to avoid the conflicts caused by profit-mongering and supporting demands for higher wages and improved living conditions for workers. Loeb points out that, "when the plague first broke out in San Francisco it was considered unpatriotic to admit the fact." Thus Loeb saw the concepts of patriot and patriotism as a means by which the ruling class of a country—any country, including America—could attach a negative label to any ideas that were contrary to the self-interests of said ruling class. So the terms were used as a way of suppressing ideas! Interestingly, Loeb was not content simply to criticize "patriotism" and "patriots"; instead, he was willing to argue in a positive fashion that "real statesmanship consists in the application of the results of the exact sciences . . . to the welfare of human society."[36]

While his friend Veblen's view of patriotism was almost entirely negative, Loeb suggested that patriotism could be understood in a more positive manner, but he qualified his remarks to Eastman in this way:

> But governments are selected from a different class and if to their ignorance is added military swagger or megalomania, wars are declared on occasion—and in that case it is patriotic to murder and be murdered for the maintenance in office and perpetuation of power of the present type of "statesman," . . . It occurs to me that by patriotism you may possibly mean the saluting of the flag by school children and the boy scout movement. If this surmise is correct I beg leave to say that I do not believe in patriotism.[37]

---

36. Loeb to Max Eastman, 10 December 1915.

37. Ibid. Still further expressions of Loeb's attitudes toward "patriotism" are found in his correspondence with Professor Julius Stieglitz, a chemist at the University of Chicago.

> I do not think that Cattell's action had had anything to do with the cruel treatment he has received from the hands of the Trustees of Columbia University since on two or three occasions before the war the same thing had been attempted by them but was prevented by the opposition of the faculty. The war was simply severely utilized by these men to overcome the objection of a number of faculty members. I think the saddest part of it is that patriotism has been used once more for selfish ends, and I think that is about as deplorable as the unnecessary cruelty of cutting Cattell off from the possibility of a pension. I suppose you are aware of the fact that his dismissal makes him ineligible for a pension from the Carnegie Institution.

Loeb to Stieglitz, 16 October 1917.

The end results of nationalism and patriotism did not escape Loeb's attention after the war, although he found them difficult to explain on rational grounds. In June, 1920, in a letter to the physicist Wolfgang Pauli, Loeb expressed surprise and chagrin at the level of interpersonal hostility that persisted, even between scientists, due to personal positions taken during the war. He had hoped to arrange visits to the United States by Austrian scientists, those he considered "not the reactionary type." He was forced to reconsider, however, not because of the attitudes or behaviors of the individuals themselves but because of their nationality and the general low regard of American scientists for colleagues from the former Central Powers. Loeb's explanation for this state of affairs was "that so many of the German professors openly sided with the Hohenzollerns" and were thus "still very reactionary." Loeb professed to have "learned to forgive my friends for the fact that they lost their reason during the war." However, he reasserted in this communication that he "was and have remained a pacifist and I have never faltered for one moment in that respect." In these comments, Loeb seems to disregard his wartime letters to his son Leonard expressing support for Wilson's position and arguing forcefully that "employees of the government" should purchase liberty bonds.[38] Like the intellectual heir of the Enlightment that he was, Loeb had difficulty accepting unreason and explaining its persistence among very well-educated people. Due to his radical social philosophy he could account for it, however, on structural grounds as being institutionally induced and culturally reinforced rather than caused by individual moral or mental weakness.

GERMAN MILITARISM

Loeb's views on the origins of the World War I were forcefully presented in his correspondence and undoubtedly also in his conversations with friends, colleagues and family. He made no bones about his dislike for the Hohenzollern regime and German militarism, although he was also well aware of the unsavory machinations of the Russian government. Interesting, too, was his explanation about how to avoid another major conflagration in the future. In the case of the present combatants involved in World War I, his focus was on the German government; he argued that the "Hohenzollern and the whole Junker regime" must be set aside as a part of any conclusion to the war. Loeb proposed its

38. Loeb to Wolfgang Pauli, 29 June 1920.

replacement by a socialist republic as he "did not think that a socialist republic [would] ever be guilty of a war." He viewed the German motivation for involvement in the war as simply a matter of the acquisition of "treasure" in particular, the mines of Belgium and northern France and possibly also "the treasures of Mexico." He stated that "A socialist republic would not act that way, but a plutocratic republic might very well be possessed by the same spirit." Turning his attention to America and the future, he expressed grave concern about that country's militaristic tendencies. Loeb did not mince words when it came to describing the effects of party politics on the probability of American involvement in military adventures. He argued that as long as the Democratic Party controlled the government in Washington, this country was unlikely to become involved in a war. However, Loeb saw the Republican Party as the instrument of business interests, exemplified by "Wall Street"; since the primary goal of those interests is profit, and since huge profits can result from war, he felt that if the Republicans gain power, "we are in danger of adopting the Prussian spirit which we are now fighting and of becoming a belligerent country in order to acquire treasure."[39]

It is also interesting to note that Loeb believed men of his own doctrinal ilk were not to blame for the war. Loeb saw himself as a "freethinker" and, of course, a mechanist. It was his conviction that such a state of mind led naturally to the support of peace, that "the freethinkers or the scientific mechanists are naturally men of peace; I could have said that it is the romanticist and the emotionalist, and not the strict mechanist, who are liable to become war-enthusiasts." Loeb acknowledged that German scientists, and presumably mechanists among them, did in fact support the war; his explanation for that state of affairs was that the German government played an active role in ensuring that only supporters of the war, or at least those who acquiesced in Junker rule, were allowed appointments to German universities.[40]

Loeb became very ambivalent regarding aspects of German culture and life. This was especially evident in his writings about German science and scientists. He argued that while German scientists saw themselves as "Teutonic super scientists," the fact was that most of their biologists were vitalists and most of their scientific effort would come to nothing of value.[41] His attitudes were shaped

---

39. Loeb to Professor Maurice Caullery, 14 May 1917.

40. Ibid.

41. Loeb to Georges Bohn, 30 March 1921.

in part by the degree to which he believed a scientific discipline had been infected by vitalism or other archaic beliefs and practices. Yet, on other occasions, Loeb seemed to feel that German science and scientists were making headway despite the difficulties imposed by the War, the postwar depression and inflation.

Loeb was very explicit about which groups and social forces had been most responsible for bringing on the War. He was also scathing in his indictment of their moral character. He wrote in retrospect that:

> I fully expected that the German Junker would try to put the blame for his having ruined Germany—and perhaps the world—on the shoulders of the Socialists and the Jews. The Junker has always been a rotten loser, and the cowardice of the Germany Emperor . . . expresses the moral status of the Junker. Their anti-Semitic propaganda is only an excuse to cover up their own stupidity and incompetence. An Englishman or an American or a Frenchman would stand his having been beaten with dignity, but the Teutonoid Junker has not got that strength of character. If Germany had been invaded and had suffered the way France did, the German government would probably have collapsed in less than a month instead of holding out for four years as the French did.[42]

One of Loeb's most extreme statements regarding German cultural achievements and world influence was made in a letter to Svante Arrhenius. The letter was written eight months before the war ended. Loeb was intent on building a postwar world and a postwar science free of the most negative influences of Germany, "their philosophy of organization, brutality, anti-Semitism." He continued that it was "imperative that we do everything to prevent the victory of the Germans over the minds of the coming generations." He was particularly concerned with the insidious effects of German science and scientific communications. He concluded that "the liberal countries like Sweden, Holland, England, America and France develop their research institution and their means of publication to such an extent that our youth is no longer compelled to look to Germany for instruction." Loeb went so far as to recommend that all of the funding for the Nobel Prizes be diverted from individual awards to the capitalization of the sciences in the western countries, the "liberal countries." He argued that the use of these funds for personal awards was a luxury that could only be afforded in the world as it existed before the war. It is apparent in this letter that after almost four years of war, Loeb felt that heroic efforts were

---

42. Loeb to Richard Goldschmidt, 16 February 1920.

necessary to salvage the free cultural and scientific institutions of the prewar world. He added, "If they want to continue giving the prizes they may do so without giving the money. If you feel my idea is correct and you wish me to agitate the matter I will greatly do so."[43] Yet, with the passage of time and the deepening of Germany's postwar economic suffering, Loeb's attitudes evolved; only a few years after the above correspondence, he commented to a German scientist that he had had several recent conversations with Abraham Flexner "about the support of those German physiologists and biologists who in my belief are doing first-class work. . . ."[44] Nevertheless, Loeb continued to harbor suspicions that the German academic community had no change of heart:

> I only hope that the Germans realize that by supporting a liberal government they can have a future; any other policy will lead to the annihilation of Germany. But I suppose you cannot preach that to the reactionaries located in the German universities. They had been rendered insane by the text books of history and tried to live up to that teutonic megalomania which Bismarck and the Kaiser have drummed into their heads.[45]

As the late war receded into the past it might have been expected that Loeb would mellow, but, as seen above, he still sounded at times like he did between 1914 and 1918, when he argued that Americans should exercise great caution in sending budding scientists to Germany for study. He feared that such long-term close association with German scientists would result in a future in which "the coming generation of Americans [would be] as brutal as the Germans." Furthermore, Loeb believed that the developing mechanistic science which he optimistically thought was evolving in American biology was superior to anything emerging in Germany.[46]

THE CAUSES AND CONSEQUENCES OF THE GREAT WAR

It is evident from Loeb's correspondence that he pondered long and hard over what had caused the Great War and what might be done to prevent a future one. His explanations and prognostications reveal

---

43. Loeb to Svante Arrhenius, 11 March 1918.

44. Loeb to Otto Warburg, 26 July 1922.

45. Loeb to Richard Goldschmidt, 28 January 1921.

46. Loeb to C. H. Parker, 11 March 1918.

a considerable degree of both political reflection and sociological sophistication for a scientist. In a series of letters to L. Hollinsworth Wood written in 1915, as the war was moving into its second year, Loeb discussed three factors, each of which in his opinion played a role in the initiation of wars in general and this war in particular. First, he discussed the effects of developing and maintaining a standing professional army. In such a situation, there develops within the society a military class ("military caste" was Loeb's way of phrasing the notion); the self-interest of this segment of society is well served by involvement in war. Loeb argued that during peacetime the military establishment is "chafing under the boredom of garrison duty. When the Mexican trouble began the graduating class of West Point voted unanimously for war. It means promotion." Therefore, at a time of international tension, this group of citizens argues for war; furthermore their families, friends and acquaintances are encouraged to support a war option, it being the patriotic thing to do. "In this fact lies in my opinion one of the greatest dangers for an increase of the army and navy during times of peace." Loeb cited Russia, Germany and France and countries which maintained "enormous armies" with the result that in each case "the entire citizenry was continuously exposed to the ferment action of the war spirit of the military caste." The reader will once again note Loeb's propensity for injecting scientific analogy into his own political ruminations, a tendency of which he was evidently well aware: "The army and navy may be considered as a ferment for war and given biological reactions the rate of fermentation is proportional to the number of ferment molecules . . . in this case . . . the numbers of soldiers . . . pardon a biologist for selecting biological analogies."[47]

In a subsequent letter that year, Loeb discussed a second cause of war, often referred to by him in other communications as "the profit motive" and related factors. Loeb advocated vehemently that all means for the manufacture of armaments should be held under state ownership. Private ownership, he argued, led to enormous profits which led in turn to tremendous political influence and this, in turn, to a contamination of the political and diplomatic moves involved in decisions of war and peace. He added that "it becomes more and more obvious that the problem of war and peace is linked inseparably with the economic problem and we shall have peace only if we get state ownership of armament factories."[48]

As glimpsed in these letters, Loeb's expressions of political

47. Loeb to L. Hollingsworth Wood, 9 February 1915.

48. Ibid., 15 August 1915.

and cultural pessimism, including the possibility of more wars, became more and more pronounced as the war continued; after the War it reached a crescendo as Loeb told colleague after colleague that the only way he could bear life any longer was to withdraw from worldly affairs and bury himself in his work. These assertions notwithstanding, Loeb never withdrew from active observation, involvement, and commentary.

A third factor increasing the likelihood of war in Loeb's view was the very act of preparing for the eventuality of war. When a nation strengthens and modernizes its forces it may be doing so strictly out of a sense of insecurity and a perceived need for self defense. A neighboring country observing these military activities, however, might itself see a need for increased readiness, and a third nation observes the second and then the first nation once again perceives its own military as inadequate to meet the new "threats" and so on. At some point one of the countries believes it cannot afford the spiraling costs of this recurring cycle and feels compelled to attack its neighbor before it is too late—and so, war. In another letter to Wood, Loeb tells of a German relaying the perception of that country that "Germany could not much longer delay war against Russia because Russia was improving and modernizing its army. . . . France saw itself endangered by the preparedness of Germany. . . . England became panicky over Germany's naval preparedness . . . France's preparedness under the two Napoleon's made Germany panicky, and etc., interminably."[49]

Early on, Loeb, who was a fascinated but horrified observer of the European conflagration, made some shrewd observations about still another cause of the War and possible changes that might be made to avoid a recurrence. The problem as Loeb saw it was the well established practice of secret bilateral diplomacy and the secret agreements that arose therefrom. "The people in all these countries are the duped" he declared, because it is the ordinary citizen who suffers the costs and casualties which result from the hidden machinations and manipulations. The solution was for the people to deny their governments the power to engage in secret treaties or even to acquire armaments. He recommended instead the formation of an international armed force which, "might be maintained for police duty." Loeb saw the efforts of the Germans, English and others to depict their own involvement in the conflict as justifiable as "ludicrous." Only the Russian Socialists were behaving correctly by refusing to join the Allies and, instead, focusing their hostility on the Russian autocracy since the latter

---

49. Ibid., 26 November 1915.

were "oppressing their own people to such an extent that the Russian Socialists have no other fight before them but the abolition of that autocracy."[50] Although at times Loeb's political analysis does not rise above the level of conventional political journalism the above statement is quite prescient considering the time in which it was written. In it, Loeb not only anticipates Woodrow Wilson's strictures against secret diplomacy and his support of "open covenants, openly arrived at"; he is also aware of the role of Russian radicals at work in what was to become the Russian Revolution.

At this early stage of the War, Loeb at times, found little to choose between the combatants and he also feared the repression of dissidents which, of course, had already begun.

> I am afraid you will be very much offended with me for expressing such views, because from the letters I receive from Germany it is as dangerous today to criticize the German government as Shaw has found it dangerous to criticize the English government. I think Sir Edward Grey is since Bismarck the most unscrupulous statesman Europe has had. Marx prophesied in 1870 that if Bismarck dared to take Alsace-Lorraine from France he would drive France into the arms of Russia and thereby provoke a further and more terrible war than of 1870. Marx's prophecy has become only too true and it can safely be prophesied that Sir Edward Grey's efforts will continue the "noble" work of Bismark and lay the foundation for the next and perhaps still more terrible war than this one.[51]

Loeb displayed an insensitivity toward the difference between British and German domestic policy with regard to treatment of wartime dissenters, as bad as the British record sometimes was, and he showed even less discrimination between the diplomacy of Bismark and Grey. Indeed, many diplomatic historians would probably have difficulty in taking seriously the latter comparison. Nevertheless, during the War and the immediate postwar era, Loeb was often astute in his judgments of the actions of diplomats and politicians and courageous in his defense of dissenters. He spared no one who attempted to repress dissent and social change, although he appeared slightly paranoid at times. For instance, Loeb expressed anger and consternation when an editorial in the *New York Evening Post* criticized a specific individual for not agreeing to participate in poison gas preparation; he, the individual was labeled by the editorial as unpatriotic. In a 1920 letter to a friend, Loeb

50. Loeb to Alice and Justus Galle, 4 December 1914.

51. Ibid.

claimed that the editorial was motivated by some conspiratorial effort by the newspaper owner "a Mr. [Thomas] Lamont, a member of the firm of international bankers, J. Pierpont Morgan and Co." Since it was rumored that the American government was manufacturing poison gas, perhaps such dissenters were being publicly attacked in order to forestall public resistance to the government activities, Loeb suggested, and he concluded that "the trouble with humanity is the ease with which the masses can be rendered insane."[52]

---

52. Loeb to William B. Brierley, 14 December 1920.

CHAPTER FOUR
LOEB'S POLITICAL
AND SOCIAL ACTIVISM

———————◆•◆———————

INTRODUCTION

Strewn through Loeb's correspondence are many letters which attest to his altruistic and charitable impulses. These include numerous donations to worthy causes; indeed, it appears that Loeb rarely turned down a request for funds that had merit and it should be kept in mind that he was not a wealthy man. He was a secular humanist, who not only advocated income redistribution through government auspices, but also accepted the obligation to give part of his own income to causes and individuals who, in his view, had a moral claim on the income stream of the community including privately held wealth.

Loeb was a strong and consistent advocate of international cooperation within the scientific community regardless of race, religion, creed or nationality. This was not mere rhetoric, for his correspondence reveals much activity on his part to promote such ends. These included joint sponsorship and support of journals and monographs, professorial appointments and exchanges, continuous free exchange of scientific information and joint research efforts. Indeed, as much of his correspondence was directed abroad as to his own domestic colleagues and he rarely failed to "pass the hat" for a scientist in need.

Loeb also had a long and, at times, strenuous involvement in social and political reform movements.[1] Most of this was an expression of his secular humanism and the doctrinal underpinnings of it are not difficult to establish. However, his affiliation with the Rockefeller Institute made him cautious at

1. A partial listing of organizations toward which Loeb appears to have been sympathetic, meaning he either joined, propagandized for, solicited membership in, or contributed money to would include at a minimum the following: Committee of One Hundred (supporting federal regulation of public health) (1907), Life Extension Institute (1913), Japan Society of America (1914), Society to Eliminate Economic Causes of War (1914-15), Single Tax (1915), Rationalist Press Association (1918), American Friends of German Democracy (1918-19), Emergency Society in Aid of European Science and Art (1920), and Committee of the American Society of Naturalists on Cooperation with the National Research Council.

times in lending his name to certain controversial causes. One such issue was artificial birth control or contraception. In December 1920, Margaret Sanger, chairman of The First American Birth Control Conference requested that Loeb provide information concerning his birth order among his siblings, that is, was he first born, or seventh or whatever the case. The significance of this information in regards to the birth control controversy was that anti-control elements, among them many Roman Catholics, had argued that most individuals of prominence in their respective fields were born late in the order of children. As part of her request Sanger assured Loeb that in any use that was to be made of the information he provided, his personal identity would not be disclosed.[2] Loeb, of course, was the oldest son in his family which vitiated Catholic claims and he did consent to the issuance of this statement: "The present data at hand in biology do not indicate that the mental capacity increases with the serial number of the offspring." But in replying to Sanger, he was careful to request that he not be identified in either the birth order information or as the source of the statement; he suggested that the statement be attributed to "a biologist." Loeb attributed his request for anonymity to his position at the Rockefeller Institute; he apparently felt the institute was better positioned if seen as taking a neutral position in regard to such issues of the day.[3] His circumspection in all this is probably testimony to the lasting effects of wartime and postwar repression of freedom of expression in the United States as well as to his pragmatism in adjusting to the realities of the political power of the Roman Church.

ALCOHOLISM, TEMPERANCE AND PROHIBITION

One of the most salient political issues of the early 20th century in the United States was Prohibition. About half of the American states were dry at the time we entered the Great War and war time economic needs limited the availability of materials for the production of alcoholic beverages. Loeb was well aware of the problems caused by the consumption of alcohol and responded positively to Irving Fisher's request that he join the Committee of Sixty whose avowed aim was national prohibition. In a series

2. Genevieve Grandcourt [Sanger's correspondent] to Loeb, 21 December 1921.

3. Loeb to Genevieve Grandcourt, 27 December 1921.

of letters to Fisher that spanned the year 1916, Loeb clarified and restated his position concerning prohibition and alcoholism; it was an evolving position as can be seen even in the letters of that one year. Loeb was initially enthusiastic about joining the Committee of Sixty because he shared the belief that social progress could be more readily realized in the absence of heavy alcohol consumption by the working poor. This Committee of Sixty was made up of prominent religious leaders, writers, speakers academics and scientists—far too few of the latter to suit Loeb. His primary initial criticism of the movement was the heavy, indeed, dominating, influence of religious groups and extremists. He argued that what was needed as a centerpiece of the movement was a broad educational campaign. He suggested that such a campaign can only succeed if carried out by "men of calm judgment and not by enthusiasts." He also argued that an educational program requires the heavy involvement of a preponderance of men of science, concluding "I feel strongly that the right type of scientific men should be secured."[4]

Not too surprisingly, Loeb had second thoughts on both the social equity and political feasibility of enforced abstinence from alcohol. In a subsequent letter dated 3 April 1916, he declined Fisher's recent suggestion that Loeb serve as a vice president for the Committee of Sixty. His reasons were that while he had strongly supported the idea of prohibition and continued to do so, he felt that too much stress was being placed on the notion of prohibition as a set of laws imposed from the top down upon the working man. He would rather identify with a movement that was more uplifting in arguing for reform from the bottom-up by means of wage increases, cost of living reductions and general reform of the standard of living of workers and their families. Given their brutal living conditions, workers had little else to turn to than the saloon as a "social center" and "short heaven" in Loeb's view. Once again he was critical of the role of religion in the whole matter when he said, "to take the saloon away and give him nothing instead except possibly more promises for a happy hereafter to keep him satisfied with his slavery, seems to me a wrong way of handling the problem." Once again Loeb repeated his oft-made observation that "prohibition has never interfered with the alcohol consumption of the well-to-do, but it has deprived the poor of his only chance of human sociability."[5] Although Loeb

---

4. Ibid., 14 January 1916.

still professed to favor prohibition and asked that his name remain on the list of the Committee of Sixty, he indicated his belief that "prohibition, if it is not accompanied by a positive movement for the improvement of the social conditions of the masses, is about as much of curse in one direction as a benefit in the other."[6]

Loeb was generally hostile toward institutional religion in any case, which clearly affected his attitudes toward prohibition since conservative religionists were backing the prohibition amendment. On 21 November 1916 he wrote Fisher that:

> A few months ago I was surprised to find that the most prominent employers of labor in New York have invited Billy Sunday to enter upon a revival campaign here. It was not difficult to understand that the real mission of that clown was that of a spiritual strike breaker. I am becoming tired of the efforts of reforming the workingman by Billy Sunday and by enforcing upon him restrictions instead of doing the decent thing, giving him a chance for a happy and decent home and thus depriving him of the necessity of the saloon and of the antics of Billy Sunday. I write to you because I know that you surely sympathize with me, but I feel that the prohibition movement attacks the evil at the wrong end.[7]

Loeb's interest in the liquor question was obviously not based on religious or moral grounds, but rather on physiological premises and considerations of social efficiency and social equity. Although it was not always easy once he became involved in the temperance movement, he did try to distance himself from the more rabid prohibitionists whose main reason for participation was moral and religious.[8] Perhaps the most interesting participant in the national dialogue over alcohol and the most frequent correspondent with Loeb on this issue was the aforementioned Fisher, an eminent neoclassical economist at Yale, who was an ardent advocate of nationwide prohibition. Fisher, who undoubtedly had moral and perhaps religious reasons for advocating total abstinence, also marshaled arguments drawn from the marginalist doctrine in

5. Ibid., 3 April 1916.

6. Ibid., 25 April 1916.

7. Ibid., 21 November 1916.

8. "I think the whole movement would have succeeded better if it had not been so exclusively in the hands of church members and fanatics." Loeb to Irving Fisher, 14 January 1916.

economics. In a letter dated November, 1916 Fisher explained his own stance on prohibition to Loeb in this manner:

> As you know I am interested in all efforts to improve the lot of workingmen and do not think that prohibition by any means is the only line of attack. Nevertheless so far as it goes I believe prohibition will add to the joy of the workingmen, not subtract, and that indirectly it will raise wages materially by increasing productivity which lies at the source of wages. In spite of some exploitation and the existence of arbitrary control over wages, to a certain extent the general wage level, as Professor Moore of Columbia and others have shown, rests on what we economists call marginal productivity of labor and this is materially improved by prohibition.[9]

While Fisher's analyses might appear valid to other proponents of marginal productivity theory in a narrow sense, it ignored most of the cultural and psychological reasons why blue-collar workers consumed alcohol in the first place. Loeb articulated this in a letter written to former Governor E. N. Foss of Massachusetts. Loeb used as an analogy the medical model in which symptoms are differentiated from underlying causes when dealing with an ill patient; it is axiomatic that the physician treat causes not symptoms. Loeb saw that many benefits would result from any successful, "movement to abolish drunkenness." However, he saw the use of alcohol as a symptom of the underlying conditions of workers, whom he viewed as an underclass of individuals living in wretched brutalizing conditions; they were underpaid and forced to endure marginal living facilities. Given the low quality of their day-to-day lives, "the poor exploited workers . . . in their present misery [find] the saloon and alcohol may be a dispeller of sorrows." Loeb argued in favor of "a positive program" which begins with an effort to provide significantly increased wages and a decent standard of living. He argued that "the prohibition movement if not accompanied by a positive program for ameliorating the economic conditions and for providing better homes for the working man is working against rather than for the happiness of mankind." Without accompanying reforms, Loeb saw prohibition as simply the addition of a "moral tyranny" to a preexisting economic tyranny. With some element of sarcasm, Loeb pointed out that "the prohibition movement never reaches alcoholism among the rich, and, as far as I can see, nobody worries about drunkenness in the so-called upper classes." He says quite clearly that he is willing to

---

9. Irving Fisher to Loeb, 23 November 1916.

lend his name and stature to a prohibition movement which states that its first goal is to alleviate the poverty and suffering of the workers. Otherwise, "I regret to say that I cannot lend my name to the movement."[10]

Loeb engaged in discussions of the liquor problem with international correspondents as well; but, again, his views must be distinguished from those with merely economic or religious motives. In a 1912 letter to an acquaintance, Loeb expressed support for the formation "of an international institute for the investigation of the effect of alcohol, from the viewpoint of individual and general hygiene and sociology." He expressed a willingness to begin the search in this country for support and funding for such an endeavor. He expressed some pessimism at the idea of finding scientific support in America for such a venture, either from individuals or from the Rockefeller Institute Board of Directors. The problem in the U.S., he goes on to say, is that in this country the idea of temperance is very often associated with a sort of religious idealism "and a fanatic ignorance manifested by a great many of these religious anti-alcohol societies that has aroused the antipathy of physicians and scientific people in general." Loeb then suggests that an independent research institute could be formed and that raising money for such an endeavor might not be difficult.[11]

Indeed, he was so interested in the anti-alcohol movement abroad that he felt obliged to make suggestions to foreign colleagues as to where they might obtain support for efforts to reduce the public's intake of alcohol and increase its awareness of the dangers of excessive drinking. Loeb was convinced that money could be raised in America for such purposes and he started off by pointing to the Rockefeller Foundation as a prime potential source. The Rockefellers had already contributed a hundred million dollars and if the U.S. Congress cooperated in making contributions to a broad effort, Loeb believed that the Rockefellers would contribute even more. "They are anti-alcoholists themselves and are deeply interested in humanitarian problems . . . look forward with a fair degree of confidence towards getting help in America, although naturally I can only speak as an individual and not officially."[12]

Loeb remained critical, nonetheless, of religionists in the temperance movement despite his acquiescence in the role of the Baptist Rockefellers who were his employers. It is interesting to

---

10. Loeb to ex-Gov. E. N. Foss, 21 November 1916.

11. Loeb to A. Holitscher, January, 1912.

12. Ibid., 23 October 1912.

note, however, that he was also critical of an entirely different participant in the anti-alcohol movement, namely, the Czar of Russia's own government. Loeb helped alert other participants in the fight against alcohol regarding the deceitful role of the Russians who, through a diplomatic agent, initiated the formation of an organization to research alcoholism. While this new organization was of a temperance character he claimed that its true intent was to disrupt such movements. The motivation was that the Russian government earned huge sums of money per year through the manufacture and sale of alcoholic beverages.[13] Throughout his battles over the liquor trade Loeb was thus politically aware in his judgments regarding the different motives of the participants and shrewd in his appraisal of their programs.

Loeb was not alone, however, in his analyses of the relationship between the temperance movement and social reform. In fact, Foss expressed strong agreement with Loeb's arguments that any movement toward prohibition must be accompanied by major social reforms including (but not limited to) "higher wages, better working conditions, economic readjustments." However, Foss pointed out, all of these progressive moves were being stoutly resisted by what he labeled "the alcohol capital" which he identified as "the great concentrations of capital in the United States . . . [under the control or influence of] . . . the saloon politicians of our centers of population." This group resists all manner of social improvement including emancipation of women, elimination of child labor and the like; furthermore, the problem exists in advanced countries around the world.[14] It is thus possible to link reformist political doctrine of a particular kind with the temperance movement, although it was certainly true that many progressives were not advocates of prohibition or anything resembling it.

Loeb's objections to the heavy use of alcohol had a scientific physiological basis rather than a moral or religious foundation. One of the best and most succinct statements of this view is found in a letter he wrote in 1920 after the Prohibition amendment was ratified. In this communication Loeb acknowledges that alcohol is used in the body as a form of food; that is, it is used as a metabolic energy source. Loeb argues, however, the negative consequences of alcohol more than neutralize its slight energy contribution. He points out that alcohol has a particularly strong capacity to disrupt activities in the nervous system. Loeb further argues that the most

13. Loeb to Jerome Greene, 17 February 1913.

14. Eugene Foss to Loeb, 29 November 1916.

serious consequence of alcohol abuse is its "injurious effect on the sex cells which makes the offspring of parents addicted to alcohol mentally and bodily inferior to that of total abstainers. This fact is of the greatest importance." He thought there was sufficient evidence to conclude that the majority of newborns with mental or physical deficiencies were attributable to the excessive consumption of alcohol by one or both parents.[15] Loeb's prescience regarding the effects of alcohol on the unborn is important considering what is now known concerning fetal alcohol syndrome, even if he was incorrect in regard to the genetic basis of the damage. Scientists after Darwin and Huxley had long suspected such a relationship existed, but few had stated it as forcefully as Loeb or with his scientific authority.

Armaments, Disarmament and Neutrality

Loeb had been skeptical regarding the European arms race and system of military alliances long before the Great War erupted. When war finally started on a grand-scale with massive bloodletting on the two main fronts, he soon became involved in overtly political efforts to keep the United States out of it. Loeb's papers indicate that he was sympathetic toward a number of the organizations that sprang up to combat our involvement in the War. He differed from many other scientists in that he was not complacent or indifferent regarding U.S. participation for Loeb was a member of the American League to Limit Armaments and circulated information from that organization to friends and acquaintances. By the middle of 1915 he was becoming increasingly alarmed that America was sliding inevitably toward involvement in the war. In a letter to L. H. Baekeland dated 20 May 1915 he expresses alarm at the risks of war. He cites conversations with Abraham Flexner, his superior at the Rockefeller Institute, who has "a chance to know the opinions of our leading financiers." Loeb reports that such evidence suggests war is "unavoidable." He further suggests that "we all must act at once, and I beg you to do all you can to help in this cause."[16]

Loeb apparently joined or supported four antiwar organizations, at least for a time, starting with the American League to Limit Armaments, which was organized to combat the spread of militarism in the United States. It was to use its influence to

15. Loeb to Aristide Rieffel, 4 September 1920.

16. Loeb to L. H. Baekeland, 20 May 1915.

promote a sane national policy for the preservation of international law and order with minimal reliance upon force. A bit later Loeb joined the Neutral Conference Committee which urged the U.S. government to call or cooperate in a conference of neutral nationals which would offer joint mediation to the belligerents by proposals calculated to form the basis of a permanent peace. In 1917 he joined the Emergency Peace Federation whose avowed purpose was to persuade Congress and the President not to declare war. Finally, the same year he contributed to the People's Council for America for Democracy and Peace which included some of the earlier antiwar organizations such as the Emergency Peace Federation and aimed at protecting the rights of labor and dissenters against U.S. involvement in the War. There was no denying Loeb's sincerity at this point in opposing U.S. entry into the War, however inconsistent his later behavior might seem.

THE SCIENTIST IN POLITICS

That Loeb belonged to the political Left is apparent in his correspondence. The question is what kind of radical was he? Although this question cannot be definitively answered here, Loeb's relationship with the avowedly socialist *New Review: A Critical Review of International Socialism* is important in explaining his larger political perspective. Its editors included W. E. B. Du Bois, Max Eastman, Floyd Dell, Robert Lowie and William English Walling among others, while its advisory council included Charlotte Perkins Gilman, Harry Laidler, Gustavus Myers, and Charles Steinmetz, names that will be familiar to those who are knowledgeable about the history of American socialism prior to the Russian Revolution. While Loeb subscribed to the *New Review* and occasionally wrote for it, he refused, in these revealing words, to join its staff:

> I have received your letter of May 5th in which you were good enough to propose my name as one of the contributing editors to the *New Review*. If the *New Review* were a purely scientific journal, I should not hesitate to allow my name to go on the board of contributing editors, but the contents of the *New Review* are outside the line of my expert knowledge. It is impossible for me to assume any kind of responsibility for publications in a domain in which I am a layman. Moreover, it may happen at any time that things will be advocated in the *Review* to which I might be utterly opposed. Under the

circumstances I hope you will pardon me if I beg you not to put my name on the list of contributing editors.[17]

This letter is revealing because once more Loeb argues that he cannot directly lend his name as a scientist to a journal that is political in nature because its focus lies outside the realm of his expert knowledge. The nature of Loeb's "radicalism" is thus clarified to the extent that it excludes scientists from posing as experts on political matters. It also seems to require that, although scientists may take stands on partisan issues, they do so as interested laymen, not as specialists giving expert witness. Had Loeb consistently adhered to this position, it would be easier to understand his behavior, but he did not. To illustrate, he wrote to the secretary of the American Neutral Conference Committee in 1916 to tell her of his willingness to be a part of a group whose aim it was to foster an international conference of neutral actors. He added his opinion that as far as the combatant countries were concerned their war aims were dictated by their respective foreign offices. He exclaimed that the resources consumed in the pursuit of the war could, if conserved for useful purposes, have solved the myriad problems faced by the entire world or as he put it, "The continuation of the war serves no ideal except that of murder."[18]

What seems on the surface to be an inconsistency in the application of Loeb's principles, however, may not be so glaring if the role of the scientist as political advocate is more closely scrutinized. Apparently, what Loeb really meant in warning against partisanship and advocacy is that the scientist *qua* scientist should not engage in such behavior when posing as a scientist in a role requiring a particular kind of expertise such as, for example, physiology or colloid chemistry. He did not mean to suggest that scientists as citizens should not engage in partisanship or advocacy so long as they did not claim to be experts on the issues on which they took a stand.

To illustrate the point further, Loeb was asked in 1920 to endorse Herbert Hoover for president of the United States. This request came from a doctor at the Cornell University Medical College in New York City who proposed to send the endorsement to 300 members of the Harvey Society who "represent the best class of physicians in the city."[19] Loeb's answer to this request may be

17. Loeb to William English Walling, 11 May 1914.

18. Loeb to Rebecca Shelly, 21 July 1916.

19. Graham Lusk to Loeb, 7 May 1920.

evidence of the freedom he believed scientists should enjoy to engage even in partisan politics. Loeb not only agreed to support Hoover's candidacy but also gave permission for the use of his (Loeb's) name in support of Hoover in any way appropriate. He expressed the opinion that Hoover's election was necessary not only for the country but also for "humanity," a ringing endorsement indeed![20]

A good illustration of Loeb's perception of his role as a scientist in politics can be found in his response to a woman who asked him about vivisectionism. This was clearly an area about which Loeb knew a great deal having experimented with animals for forty years. He was also aware of the politically inflammatory nature of the subject. Loeb took great pains to explain to this inquirer that science goes to great length to avoid inflicting unnecessary pain on experimental animals. He pointed out that it would be as impossible to conduct surgery on an unanesthetized dog as it would be to do so on an unanesthetized human. Those cases in which anesthesia is not used on dogs, he explained, were procedures in which anesthesia would also not be used with humans, as in the case of vaccination. As he put it "I do not think it is more cruel to vaccinate a dog than to vaccinate a human being." In very blunt terms he went on to say that, "antivivisectionists have been exploited by adventurers, who, finding them gullible victims, have supplied them with the most fantastic and untruthful statements." Loeb further opined that, if medicine and physiology were denied the use of experimental animals, medicine would revert to its status in the Middle Ages. He attributed the extremist sentiments of some antivivisectionists to the fact that "the curse of the human race is that they are guided by emotions—very often of an irrational type— rather than reason."[21]

INSTITUTIONAL RELIGION AND SECULAR HUMANISM

Loeb's views on institutional religion and especially the Christian churches, were closely linked with his espousal of what has subsequently come to be known as "secular humanism." The linkage between the two is articulated in his correspondence with a high degree of consistency and it is impossible to understand his antipathy, for example, toward Roman Catholicism or

---

20. Loeb to Graham Lusk, 10 May 1920.

21. Loeb to Sara C. Harkness, 28 October 1919.

fundamentalism without recognizing that it is rooted in an atheistic materialism that is itself based on an entirely different view of the nature and destiny of humankind.

First, however, let us examine his analysis and mockery of institutional religion before we turn to his alternative to it, namely, secular humanism. Loeb's comments are both focused, sardonic and, at times, inflammatory:

> Just as I see only one duty to perform in the case of Billy Sunday's revival meetings, either to ignore them or if one participates to point out the lack of harmony of that emotionalism with our present state of knowledge and civilization. For these reasons I can honestly give only one advice and that is not to offer any so-called help, which as a matter of fact is not needed. . . . This, of course, is not the reason that induces me to advise you, but as I stated my protest against the homicidal emotionalism which seems to pervert many human minds.[22]

However, it is interesting to note that Loeb, despite his mordant denunciations of institutional religion, did not always lose his sense of humor about it.

> One good turn is worth another; after the invitation you sent me I am going to retaliate with sending you an application blank for membership in the Religious Education Association. If you read over the literature I send with it you will see that the advantages connected with such membership are quite considerable. The question which our friend Swain is discussing, "Does God Have a Body," has interested me for some time and I intended to have a chapter on that in my book but somehow I got scared at the idea that if Haeckel is right and the body is gaseous whether it would be proper to call it a body. Since I have no time to come to New Haven I think you might do me the favor to consult the Ref. Swain and tell him of my trouble, for I see that questions are answered after each address. I am sure you will be enlightened.[23]

Loeb did not confine his attacks on institutional religion to religious fundamentalism, however. His contempt for the Roman Catholic Church probably exceeded his dislike of biblical literalism. Indeed, he was fond of claiming that his books were on the Index of the Catholic Church and used this as an example of the

---

22. Loeb to R. E. Skeel, 23 October 1910.

23. Loeb to Richard Goldschmidt, 16 February 1917.

incompatibility of science and religion. He commented that "the one arch enemy humanity has is ignorance of science and the rule of the Catholic Church which perhaps go hand in hand."[24]

Loeb's mechanistic materialist philosophy was at odds with the religiosity which permeated American evangelicalism. It is evident, however, in his correspondence that he apparently disliked Roman Catholicism as much or more than he did fundamentalism. In a letter to John D. Rockefeller, Jr., he reflected on his experiences as a child growing up in a German town on the banks of the Rhine. The great majority in the town was Roman Catholic while the small minority was made up of Protestants and Jews—Loeb being of the latter group. Loeb is revealing of the formative factors in his own life when he states, "My early experience in life has taught me to be fearful of the church when it becomes too powerful" and "I can assure you that the life of every non-Catholic child, Protestant and Jew alike, was made a burden." Briefly, he goes on to describe the nature of interactions that led to his discontent in that town. Loeb concludes that "humanistic science, developed on the safe basis of exact experiments, is a much gentler master than an organized church."[25] He perceives that Americans who have not had such experiences will have difficulty understanding his point of view.

Loeb, then, did not simply dislike institutional religion because he considered its creeds and doctrines to be false, although this was an important factor. He believed the tyrannical potential of the church to be considerable especially when one denomination was in the majority. He also considered religion to be a tool of the vested interests and projected a dismal outcome of the Great War. In a letter to his son Robert in March of 1918 he saw the war as "a war of greed," fought only to satisfy the desire for profit on the part of "the usurers and money lenders, the big industrialists and that gang." At the completion of the war he predicted little outcome beyond ruin and devastation. He argued that religion and organized churches had little to offer in the way of preventing future wars; he saw religion and "the Billy Sundays" as forces bent on the exploitation of humanity. Loeb did see, however, an eventual salvation for humanity and that salvation rested in science. He maintained a conviction that after the war science would return to its upward path of developing an understanding of physical and chemical laws which he saw as the underlying basis of all life phenomena. The benefits of such a quantitative exact science would grow slowly but steadily. Loeb felt that when social decisions

---

24. Loeb to D. R. Netter, 10 December 1918.

25. Loeb to John D. Rockefeller, Jr., 24 May 1918.

are based on the knowledge derived from science the result will be to democratize all aspects of society "so that the time will come when the money lenders, organized priesthood, and all kings and Junkers, . . . will be put out of business."[26] Since this letter was written to his son, Loeb's unflattering indictment of the military and political-religious complex was an unusually candid one which might not have been expressed so virulently to an outsider he did not trust.

It would be a serious error to conclude, however, as a religionist might, that Loeb had no moral or philosophical alternatives to religious belief and practice. On the contrary, he was an articulate and deeply committed secular humanist as a message to his former Chicago colleague the well-known psychologist-philosopher James Hayden Tufts indicated; he was writing to Tufts to thank him for a memorial volume Tufts had sent him containing an autobiography of his wife who had recently died. Interestingly, Loeb thanked Tufts for his omission of the phrase, "life after death." Pointing to his own inability to separate personal philosophy from scientific experience, Loeb went on to describe his own belief that with death, all existence comes to an end. This situation is the same for all life forms, plant, animal, and human. He expressed regret that all humans did not share his view of life as a brief "efflorescence." He believed that all wars and much human pain and conflict would cease as soon as people saw the brief transitory nature of existence and the futility of struggles which unnecessarily "mar the happiness which might be ours while we are alive."[27]

A few months later, Loeb wrote that "gentleness and humanitarianism are much more common among Freethinkers and even atheists than among the devout." The fact that these comments were directed to an eminent liberal Protestant minister[28] indicated that Loeb was more militant and intellectually aggressive than many secular humanists in advancing his own version of atheistic materialism. Not content simply to rebut religious doctrine as superstition, he articulated an alternative creed which he found rooted in the ethos of empirical science.

Although Loeb's occasional militancy leaves no doubt about

---

26. Loeb to Robert Loeb, 5 March 1918.

27. Loeb to James Hayden Tufts, 14 June 1920.

28. Loeb to John Haynes Holmes, 26 February 1921. Loeb's sometimes militant opposition to Roman Catholicism was particularly evident in his desire to see it driven out of Mexico. See Loeb's comments to this effect in this letter to L. H. Baekeland, 10 July 1916.

the advancement of secular humanism, he was not uncritical or dogmatic in defense of all "freethinking." Indeed, his objectivity and detachment were never more evident than in this description of a debate in which he participated.

> Anyway, in this discussion the Freethinkers, who consisted of some uneducated doctors and some laymen, exhibited a degree of ignorance and wild stupidity which contrasted most unfavorably with the very careful statement which Crew as the spokesman of the church people made. I felt ashamed of my fellow-truthseekers, and when I was called upon to make a few remarks, I told them that in science we could only take things for proven when they were based on experiments and on quantitative experiments and that from this point of view ours (that means twenty-five years ago) was not the era of Darwin but the era of Pasteur. Whereupon all my fellow-freethinkers assailed me the most violently while the clergymen patted me on the back.[29]

POLITICS OF SCIENCE

Loeb, like other politically knowledgeable scientists, was very sensitive regarding the mixture or infusion of politics into science. To illustrate this point, during the War Loeb became involved in an episode in which purely political considerations impinged on the publication of an article in a scientific journal. The issue was that an article had been submitted by a Swiss scientist; the reviewers had recommended its publication but those in charge of publication balked because the author had German institutional affiliations. In a letter to Dr. Ross G. Harrison of the Osborn Zoological Laboratory at Yale University, Loeb stated that, in his view, it was inappropriate for political considerations based on wartime animosity toward Germans to override the scientific merit of research. Loeb argued, forcefully, that scientific decisions concerning a scientific article and its suitability for publication should be reserved exclusively for the scientific board. The board overseeing publication should serve only as an agent for the scientific board. The latter should demand compliance with its decision. Loeb was, however, open to some degree of compromise on the matter; he suggested that the author's German institutional affiliations might go unmentioned on the publication, and further that the German language original be translated into English for

---

29. Loeb to E. G. Conklin, 9 January 1924.

publication. But as far as national affiliation of scientists and the relationship of those affiliations to the European conflict were concerned, Loeb was adamant, and he stated that "it is incomprehensible to me why political affairs should in any way be mixed up with the publication of statements of abstract science which is or should be above the stupidity and the brutality of politics."[30]

Loeb's commitment to pure as opposed to applied science also had "political" overtones—although this had more to do with the internal administration of medical schools than with "politics" as it is usually understood. In a May 1920 letter to A. O. Leuschner marked "confidential," Loeb lamented that departments of physiology have been made subservient to the applied science needs of medical training. The clinical work of the physician requires well–trained technicians to conduct what Loeb saw as the mundane tasks of blood pressure, pulse curves and blood, urine and feces analysis. While these tasks are important to the needs of the clinician, they do not break new scientific ground in investigating "the mechanism of life phenomena." The result was, as Loeb saw it, that chairs of departments of physiology have been filled with individuals who were sympathetic to clinical needs but not necessarily committed to the most advanced research, with the final result that many of these departments were "completely sterile and . . . fifty years behind the times."[31]

In part, of course, Loeb's complaint has to do with the "vocationalization" of physiology which in his view is rooted in a justifiable distinction between pure and applied science. Far from denigrating applied science in the training of technicians, he applauded its use in this capacity. His point was simply that failure to invest adequately in pure scientific research would have negative consequences in the future, particularly in an immature field of research like human physiology where much remained to be learned.

THE AUTONOMY OF SCIENTISTS AND INTELLECTUALS

Because of his experience with academic institutions in Hohenzollern Germany where ethnic, religious, and political criteria were often used to determine academic appointments and advancement, Loeb was very concerned to protect academics from

---

30. Loeb to Ross Harrison, 29 October 1917.

31. Loeb to A. O. Leuschner, "Confidential," 3 May 1920.

external subjugation. His contempt for intellectuals who surrendered their scientific and political autonomy on account of self-interest was, at times, scathing; witness Loeb's comments to the historian of science George Sarton:

> I enclose the part of [Hugo] Münsterberg's letter you sent to me. He is always the same grandiloquent humbug. It is very amusing that he, who represents the greatest degeneracy a scientist can reach, namely that of terminating as a journalistic money-making hack, should sit in judgment over American science or talk about the problems of history of science to be solved in this or in any other country. I have read, in connection with an address which I have foolishly promised to give at the Naturalist's meeting here on Biology and War, a good deal of the German journalistic writers of the Münsterberg type; namely among others Houston Chamberlain, [F. A. J. von] Bernhardi, [Heinrich von] Treitschke, and they all suffer from the same type of mental degeneracy which is so obvious also in Münsterberg. I think the present war is of course primarily a war of greed for gold and power, but next to that we have to thank that crop of irresponsible writers of the Münsterberg type which has arisen in Germany and which threatens to lower the mentality of the whole world in the direction of medievalism.[32]

Loeb was thus sensitive to encroachment on the autonomy of scientists by both government and business. His correspondence after World War I indicates a fear of the loss of freedom on the part of those engaged in the pursuit of scientific inquiry. His letters to Svante Arrhenius provide ample evidence of this. In a letter to him written just three months after the war, Loeb decried the perpetuation of the National Research Council beyond the end of the war, the emergency situation for which it was formed. Loeb argued that the centralization of scientific research under one organization and ultimately under one individual was bad for science as well as the individual scientists. He declared, "You can easily see what it will lead to. He will be in a position to ruin the career of any young man who for some reason or other appears obnoxious to his immediate clique."[33] Loeb's antipathy to centralization was thus an important aspect of his view that scientific

---

32. Loeb to George Sarton, 16 December 1916. For an explanation of the attitude of many academics toward Münsterberg after the start of World War I. See Jutta & Lothar Spillman, "The Rise and Fall of Hugo Münsterberg," *Journal of the History of the Behavioral Sciences*, 29 (October, 1993): 322-38.

33. Loeb to Svante Arrhenius, 4 February 1919.

research should be autonomous from the structures of power.

Loeb was quite perceptive at times as to the motives of scientists—especially those in the professoriate. In the same letter to Arrhenius, Loeb argues that many American scientists lose interest in pursuing only laboratory goals, and begin to search about for other conquests. He points out that George Hale, the first and continuing head of the National Science Foundation was, after the war, attempting to make his organization an international one. Although Hale had insured that the Americans he had selected for the committee would go along with his own expansionist notions, some scientists such as Thompson and Rutherford were resisting Hale's policy of centralized control of scientific activity. This resistance Loeb pointed to with approval; in general, however, he was pessimistic about the future of "pure science." The costs of science, he feared, would lead to centralization, and those in control would limit support to those projects in which the practical application and ultimate commercial profit were immediately apparent.[34] Loeb thus came down forcefully on the side of pure research versus applied research, as might be expected of an experimental scientist of his stature, and he remained suspicious of government control over funding of science.

Loeb's dislike of political interference with scientific work even got him involved in a minor way with the threatened removal of a federal official. In Loeb's correspondence can be found the following letter:

> Recently I learned that Secretary of Commerce Herbert Hoover had called for the resignation of Dr. Hugh M. Smith, as Commissioner of Fish and Fisheries, on the ground that the

---

34. Ibid., Loeb wrote to Ernest Rutherford on 31 August 1920 to tell him that:
   We are threatened here with a bureaucratic administration of research by the National Research Council. Hale has gotten the Carnegie money (about 120 millions, practically under his control by having one of the henchmen appointed President of the corporation, and it is intended that in the new building in Washington (for which he has already the necessary millions) an office be established to which every worker is supposed to promptly announce the subject of an investigation he may decide to start upon, so that he may be advised whether or not his work is a duplication of somebody else's or whether for other reasons he had better change his subject. This information is, of course, "voluntary" on the part of the investigator, but give a good American political machine and the money to back its will I should like to see which young men will have to stand up against it. The outlook for development of research was never especially good in American universities, but if Washington bureaucracy and politics becomes the de facto and official, one wonders what will happen. The bureaucratic positions of the National Research Council pay well and will be the Mecca of those university men who have political talent and are willing to take orders.

commercial interests were not satisfied with his administration. Dr. Smith was nominated by the Zoologists, as requested by the earlier administration, and he had the full support of the scientific men of the country. It is because he has proceeded on the basis of scientific principles that he has incurred the enmity of the commercial interests. Would it be possible for the Naturalists to submit a protest to Secretary Hoover? Concerted action in harmony with the Zoologists would be eminently desirable, I think. It is very surprising to me that Hoover, himself a trained engineer, should disregard the support given to Dr. Smith by the scientific men of the country, and should take steps to dislodge Dr. Smith from his post at the insistence of men whose sole interest is pecuniary. . . .[35]

Loeb's reply to the author was immediate and to the point; he was emphatically in favor of speedy action on behalf of the scientist involved.[36] As always, when it came to science versus politics (or scientists versus politicians), Jacques Loeb was on the side of science and the scientist. This was far more than the simplistic practice notion of "us versus them." Loeb felt deeply that the improvement of the human condition and human social institutions was only possible when decisions on any matter were based on scientific experimentation rather than speculation or politics.

Indeed, Loeb proclaimed that in certain respects government intervention and centralized control had already proceeded too far. To his colleague H. S. Jennings of John Hopkins University he wrote to express his agreement with Jennings on a matter of conflict between the National Research Council and the Committee of the American Society of Naturalists which Jennings chaired. The issue involved demands by the Research Council for increased cooperation with its guidelines. Loeb argued that his (Jennings) continued independence from the Research Council would best serve "the cause of science." He urged Jennings to hold out "against the jingoistic attitude of the National Research Council."[37]

Loeb's own stature and acquaintanceship in the realm of science late in his life was exemplified in a letter he wrote to Alexander Meiklejohn, president of Amherst College, in response to a Meiklejohn request for names of eminent physicists who might be invited to lecture at the Massachusetts school. Loeb recommended a number of Nobel Laureates in physics and it is

---

35. A. Franklin Shull to Loeb, 21 January 1922.

36. Loeb to A. Franklin Shull, 23 January 1922.

37. Loeb to H. S. Jennings, 20 April 1920.

evident that he knew several of them personally. His list included Ernest Rutherford, Lawrence Bragg, Neils Bohr, Robert Millikan, Arthur Compton and Albert Einstein.[38]

Loeb often attempted to help others, especially academics, who were in need. Some were relatively unknown, others eminent and, interestingly, Loeb did not expect anything in return for aiding them. He did not hesitate at times to use old friendships to aid those he thought worthy. One such individual was the visiting Italian nobleman Duke Litta Visconti Arese who sought Loeb's assistance in obtaining introductions to organizations and individuals who might wish to hear him lecture.

Loeb was open and generous to a fault in inviting Arese to use his (Loeb's) name in attempting to make contacts at Chicago. Loeb had lost contact with some of his acquaintances at Chicago, but he had maintained his friendship with the prominent psychologist James Roland Angell who was dean of the university and head of the department of psychology. Loeb informed Arese by letter that he would contact Angell and inform Angell of Arese's interests in lecturing at Chicago. "I advise you to communicate with him as soon as you arrive in Chicago,"[39] he suggested to Arese whom he had apparently never met. But such openness was typical of Loeb.

Loeb, also, on occasions attempted to aid Albert Einstein in the aftermath of World War I; at the time Einstein held an appointment at the University of Berlin and apparently could not obtain even the modest sums he needed for his own scientific work. Interestingly, Loeb was one of the individuals Einstein contacted in his quest for aid partly, no doubt, because of Loeb's eminence as a scientist and his connection with the Rockefeller Institute which was known in the scientific world to have money. In January 1924, Loeb communicated with his friend and colleague Dr. Abraham Flexner concerning the poor state of support for Einstein's research. In his letter to Flexner, Loeb states that "Einstein is on the verge of the solution of one of our outstanding riddles in science, the nature of the quantum theory." In those days without computers or even very sophisticated mechanical calculators, Einstein was confronted with an enormous burden of calculations before he could reach a solution to his problem. Because of the total lack of research support at the University of Berlin, Einstein, through Loeb, requested support from the Rockefeller Institute in the paltry amount of $360 to be used to hire a mathematician to assist in the calculations. Loeb suggested a more generous level of support, "I would recommend

---

38. Loeb to Alexander Meiklejohn, 15 November 1922.

39. Loeb to Duke Litta Viscounti Arese, 8 April 1912.

that he be offered an annual grant of $500 till he can complete his work."[40] Einstein did not find a "solution" to the nature of quantum theory during his lifetime, in fact he felt that, at some level, it was fundamentally flawed because it suggested the existence of a realm of acausal probabilistic events in the subatomic world. His concerns led to his now famous comment to Niels Bohr, the Danish physicist, "God does not play dice with the universe."

Loeb's own political convictions and ideological position during the early years of the war were exemplified by his ties to *The New Review* for which he occasionally wrote and to whose financial support he contributed. Loeb considered it to be "the most dignified and best socialistic monthly"[41] in the United States. A German Socialist writer, Carl Hauptmann, had submitted a paper to *The New Review* with the expectation of receiving compensation for the work. Loeb was forced to explain in return correspondence that "It was my mistake not to have mentioned that our socialistic papers here are so poor that they cannot pay any honorarium to the contributors. We keep up the *New Review* by constant financial support." Loeb suggested to Hauptmann that the piece be submitted to "one of the editors of our better type of capitalistic magazines . . . [although] . . . these magazines are at the same time all anti-German." Loeb concluded, however, by recommending that the author go ahead and publish in *The New Review* without compensation.[42]

Loeb's views on the control of the American press are telling though he was no apologist for the Hohenzollern regime, he felt that Germany was not receiving fair treatment from U.S. newspapers. Although this cannot be regarded as evidence of German nationalism, after living here for 25 years, it probably is evidence of his remaining in part a cultural German until the end of his days.

LOEB ON POLITICIANS AND POLITICS

One of the most interesting letters Loeb ever wrote was to President Theodore Roosevelt, a politician whose nationalism, bellicosity and militarism he came to loathe. However, in this letter he attempted in a simplistic way to link his laboratory work with political analysis and also argued that the most capable statesmen were those most knowledgeable about science. On 8 February 1909, while still a

40. Loeb to Abraham Flexner, 21 January 1924.

41. Loeb to Carl Hauptmann, 15 February 1915.

42. Ibid., 26 April 1915.

professor of physiology at the University of California, he wrote that:

> I believe it to be no accident that England, which produces the
> largest number of real statesmen, also leads in the number of
> eminent representatives of the experimental sciences,
> especially of physicists. Nowhere are statesmen more closely in
> touch and intimately acquainted with the fundamental sciences
> (physics, chemistry, and experimental biology) than in
> England; e.g., Salisbury and Balfour. The progressive character
> of Emperor William's [Wilhelm] government, is due to his
> appreciation of science and his close contact with the leading
> German scientists. The transition from the past to modern
> statesmanship is marked by the substitution of fertile science
> for sterile bureaucracy and jurisprudence or the limited
> horizon of the business men.[43]

Loeb's reference to Lord Salisbury and Arthur Balfour must be
regarded as somewhat disingenuous since they exemplified late
Victorian and Edwardian British Conservatism and imperialism; his
commentary on Wilhelm II's regime in Germany even more so.
Loeb then shifted away, however, from these statesmen to the real
meat of his letter which links his own work on instincts and tropisms
with social behavior and the degree to which the institutional
structure of any nation exhibits fairness and justice in dealing with
its own citizenry and with other nations. The foundation of this
discussion is Loeb's assertion that a sense of justice and fairness is in
humans, at least, a basic instinct. He then uses the assumption of the
existence of such an instinct as "the basis for an optimistic forecast
of the future of society, since no predatory influence, no corrupt
press, no bureaucratic and juristic narrowness can permanently
overpower this instinct any more than . . . mating or eating." Thus
Loeb sees this sense of justice as an innate aspect of humans that will
inevitably, sooner or later, seek expression. He then refers to his
earlier work with lower organisms in which he demonstrated that
innate capacities, such as cell division in an egg, can be brought to
expression through environmental manipulation. Of course the
prime example of his work in this area was his demonstration of what
he called "artificial parthenogenesis" in a sea urchin egg; he induced
cell division in an unfertilized sea urchin egg, a phenomenon not
previously observed, by manipulating the salt solutions bathing the
egg. While Loeb did not review the details of artificial
parthenogenesis in his letter to the president, he was clearly drawing
on his experiences in such experimental work when he asserted that

---

43. Loeb to Theodore Roosevelt, 8 February 1909.

the instinctive sense of justice in a nation can "become pre-eminent" under the appropriate conditions. Loeb is vague in describing exactly how this condition can be brought about other than "by fostering and embellishing it." He asserts that no other human instinct is more important to the emergence of national well being. He then appeals to Roosevelt's vanity by adding that "the statesman who makes it his policy to foster this instinct in the nation will win deeper and more permanent gratitude."[44] Whatever Loeb's motives in writing this letter to Roosevelt, it aroused enough interest in the latter to elicit the following response on 13 February 1909.

> Your letter interested me much, perhaps especially the sentence in which you say that "modern statesmanship is marked off from the statesmanship of the past, by the substitution of fertile science for sterile bureaucracy and jurisprudence or the limited horizon of the business man." I entirely agree with you. I am particularly pleased also by your scientific basis for the belief that we are justified in our optimism.[45]

Since Roosevelt did not know Loeb personally, it was unlikely that he had any idea that the latter was contemptuous not only of politicians generally but particularly of political leaders like himself, who exhibited bellicosity and militaristic attitudes at every opportunity while claiming to be men of peace.

Loeb became bitterly disillusioned with the results of the Versailles Peace Conference and soon thereafter with the behavior of

---

44. Ibid., On 9 February 1917 Loeb wrote to his son Robert and offered this advice:
> If by chance the boys at the fraternity should rush forward at the first call of volunteers I want you to keep cool and wait. Anyway do nothing, but tell them that you cannot do anything until you have consulted with your parents. I have such an absolute contempt for the stupidity of war that I certainly do not propose to suffer in my own family for this mental backwardness of our statesmen if I can help it. Teddie Roosevelt is in my opinion a plain paranoiac, and so are a number of the war enthusiasts; they are on par with Harry Thaw, though they may have a little more control over their paranoic instincts.

Loeb also expressed his attitudes toward Roosevelt in a letter to George S. Viereck on 11 April 1922.
> I hope you will forgive me for not having thanked you long ago for your kindness in sending me your book on "Roosevelt." I have read the book with the greatest interest, especially both your personal experiences during the war as well as your experiences with Roosevelt. You cannot expect a scientist to be an admirer of a man of Roosevelt's type. To the scientist, truthfulness is the first virtue and to the politician it is, perhaps, the last.

45. Theodore Roosevelt to Loeb, 13 February 1909.

the League of Nations. Phillip Pauly has suggested that the Great War and its aftermath so alienated Loeb from politics that he withdrew into his laboratories. What seems to have happened, however, is that he remained as interested and involved in politics as ever, but that having had his fingers burnt by politicians many times, he refused to support particular candidates for office. The eminent neoclassical economist Irving Fisher of Yale asked him to support the Democratic ticket of James M. Cox and Franklin D. Roosevelt in 1920, but Loeb wrote Fisher to inform him that he could not lend his support or endorsement to the Cox/Roosevelt ticket. He then went on in a rather negative tone to explain that, furthermore, he was no longer in support of the League of Nations because, in the form that it had come to take, presumably at the hands of manipulative politicians, the League had become "a curse to humanity." He was also hostile toward "the way in which President Wilson has allowed his Fourteen Points to be mutilated "into a monstrosity."[46] It would seem, however, that Loeb did not become politically inactive; rather, he simply shifted the focus of his political efforts away from electoral politics.

LOEB AND ACADEMIC FREEDOM

One of Loeb's most impressive traits was his willingness to defend others against infringements of their academic freedom. He was involved in several cases, two of which achieved a fair degree of notoriety; they were the cases of James McKeen Cattell, the psychologist who was fired from Columbia, and Bertrand Russell, the eminent philosopher and logician, who was relieved of his connection with Cambridge University; a third involved Gustav Mann of Tulane University. Needless to say, Loeb spent a great deal of his time and energy on the Cattell case because it was homegrown, in New York City to be precise, and because he was well acquainted with Cattell. Cattell's son had once worked as his assistant at the Marine Biological Laboratory in Woods Hole, Massachusetts.

The Cattell case has been dealt with elsewhere in some detail; our focus on it is only to analyze Loeb's role in it which was quite consistent both with his secular humanism and with his perspective on the exercise of academic freedom in the university setting. The Board of Trustees at Columbia University and President Nicholas Murry Butler claimed to have dismissed Cattell for disloyalty, that is, for making fundamental criticism of U.S. involvement in World War I. To make matters worse, his dismissal made him ineligible for a

---

46. Loeb to Irving Fisher, 11 September 1920.

pension from the Carnegie Institution. In short, Cattell lost his job, his salary and his pension ostensibly for his negative statements regarding American entry into the war even though the faculty at Columbia voted against his dismissal. Loeb's view of Cattell's firing was, however, that his statements were the occasion for his dismissal not the reason. He argued that the university administrators and trustees harbored a hostility toward Cattell and tried on previous occasions to deal with him—unsuccessfully. But with the advent of the war, Cattell's comments in opposition to the war provided an excuse for terminating him. The rationale was an alleged lack of patriotism on Cattell's part. The argument against Cattell was that anyone who did not agree with the war aims of the government at that time was by definition unpatriotic and worthy of termination. Faculty who had previously supported Cattell in other conflicts with university administrators were intimidated into silence for fear of the label "unpatriotic."[47]

Other faculty in the Eastern United States and at Columbia also protested against Cattell's dismissal. Two of them were the eminent historian Charles A. Beard, who resigned his post as a protest against Cattell's treatment, and the single most influential American philosopher John Dewey, who wrote to Loeb concerning the Cattell affair. He urged joint action by a large number of prominent academics and scientists in the form of a signed memorial to the trustees on Cattell's behalf, attesting to his long and productive service to science and to the academy in general (Cattell was at this time the editor of the prestigious journal *Science*) It is interesting to note, in light of present standards for academic free speech by tenured faculty, that the best that even so prominent an academic as Dewey could hope for was to save Cattell's pension which was administered separately by the Carnegie Institution. There was no expression of hope for saving his job![48]

Loeb appears to have been involved in at least two other cases involving academic freedom. The first involved Bertrand Russell who was dismissed from his position at Trinity College, Cambridge, England. Loeb wrote as follows to John Dewey regarding the case which grew out of Russell's disagreement with British war aims and government treatment of dissenters.[49]

---

47. Loeb to Graham Lusk, 16 October 1917, marked *"Strictly confidential."*

48. John Dewey to Loeb, 9 October 1917.

49. See Caroline Moorehead, *Bertrand Russell: A Life* (New York: Viking Press, 1993) Chap. 10; and Alan Ryan, *Bertrand Russell: A Political Life* (New York: Hill & Wang, 1988) Chap. 3.

Under the circumstances I feel that it would be almost a duty for the neutrals to help him out in the way of some appointment as lecturer here until the war is over. I have no doubt that after that time the Englishmen will come to their senses and will reappoint him again. I feel that it might perhaps be best for the time being to keep the fact of his being dropped at Cambridge a secret, since it might interfere somewhat with his appointment in those universities who toady to the English authorities. Do you think that Tufts could offer him anything in Chicago? Of course, the natural place to think of would be Harvard, but Harvard is so terribly pro-British that I am afraid there is no hope for him there for the present.[50]

The other case involving academic freedom in which Loeb became interested involved the dismissal of physiologist Gustav Mann from his post at Tulane University. Loeb probably took an interest in this case because he had earlier recommended Mann for this position and Mann complained to him when he was dismissed apparently for making comments on Ivy Day critical of the existing science curriculum for freshman and sophomores which, in his opinion, failed to prepare them for work in anatomy and physiological chemistry.[51] In a letter to Mann in August of 1915, Loeb assured him of support. He asserted that since Mann was a full professor and held that position with tenure, the university had "no right" to terminate his employment. Loeb declared that he had turned the entire matter over to an officer of the American Association of University Professors, "and am glad to say that he agrees with me in regard to the permanency of tenure." However, Loeb ended this last sentence with the phrase, "although he thinks that your address was perhaps not very judicious." Given that Mann's so-called offense was to criticize the existing science curriculum in a public forum and nothing else, it is interesting that Loeb saw fit, in the same letter, to tell Mann that other sanctions could have been more appropriate; "They might have censured you . . . they might have insisted that you not address the students [in a manner critical of faculty] or they might have forbidden your future addresses."[52] It seems clear such abridgments of free speech would be less likely to be tolerated on many American campuses today. But, it does not appear, at least in the short run, that Loeb succeeded in changing, much less reversing, the injustice done to

---

50. Loeb to John Dewey, 27 March 1916.

51. Gustav Mann to Loeb, 24 August 1915.

52. Loeb to Gustav Mann, 20 August 1915.

Cattell, Russell or Mann. Nevertheless, he played an active role in attempting to redress the grievances of three of his academic colleagues in the hopes that, even if efforts to help them failed, academic freedom and tenure would be more secure for future generations. Thus the Loeb portrayed here and by Phillip Pauly, is that of a sober and immensely energetic activist scientist who was enormously interested in and knowledgeable about political and social affairs. This is certainly an accurate portrayal of him insofar as his unpublished papers permit a generalization of this sort. Nevertheless, he was not without a sense of humor and, indeed, at times engaged in satirical mockery of the powers-that-be that gave his correspondence an even greater pungency and relevance.[53]

---

53. Loeb to Paul H. DeKruif. One such example of this was his description of the adventures of the great Russian scientist Ivan Pavlov in the United States:

> It may amuse you to learn that Professor Pavlov, after four years efforts, was given a passport to visit the United States and was given fifteen hundred dollars by the Soviet for his traveling expenses in America. He was promptly robbed of the money on one of the first days here at the Grand Central Station when he took a ticket to Boston, was the first to go into a car, was followed by three toughs who held him up and took every cent he had and all his belongings of any value, and made their departure. On the same day the papers reported that our own Dr. Finley had taken walks twenty-five miles in the outskirts of Moscow without being the least molested or troubled. So you see it is really very important that the United States be protected against the invasion from that robber association in Moscow.

In the same letter to scientist Paul DeKruif, he also commented that:

> I don't know whether you follow what is going on here. If you were here you and Mr. [Sinclair] Lewis could find beautiful examples of Babbitism among the university trustees, not only President Lowell of Harvard but also in Amherst where the liberal President Meiklejohn was fired, and in Clark where other interesting things are happening.

CHAPTER FIVE
LOEB'S INFLUENCE ON
THORSTEIN VEBLEN

———◆———

INTRODUCTION

No study presently exists that systematically traces the influence of
Loeb's thought on the American social sciences, humanities and
journalism. It would be interesting to know more about the
breadth and depth of his influence on his contemporaries,
particularly if it exemplified the impact of mechanistic
materialism and psycho-physiological reductionism on
intellectuals of certain kinds. However, more than speculation is
possible given the archival materials now available. A list of
important philosophers who knew Loeb's work and were likely to
have been influenced by him would include his Chicago
colleagues John Dewey and George H. Mead and Harvard's
William James, who repeatedly cites him in the *Principles of
Psychology* (1890). Psychologists acquainted with his work
included James Mckean Cattell, John B. Watson and Joseph
Jastrow and, perhaps, G. Stanley Hall and Ivan Pavlov.
Anthropologist Franz Boas, historian of science George Sarton,
novelists Sinclair Lewis, Upton Sinclair, Jack London and
Theodore Dreiser should be added to the list. Finally, journalists
and political analysts Herbert Croly, William English Walling,
Max Eastman, W. E. B. Dubois, and Oswald Garrison Villard knew
Loeb personally and had some familiarity with his ideas. In his
correspondence with others, H. L. Mencken makes reference to
Loeb. Another individual who knew Loeb personally was the
influential heterodox economist Thorstein Veblen (1857-1929),
who will serve here as a case study of both intellectual influence
and doctrinal convergence.

Loeb and Veblen were colleagues and friends at the University
of Chicago in its early years.[1] After Loeb left Chicago for the
University of California at Berkeley in 1902, he and Veblen
continued to correspond and visit with each other, and Loeb may

---

1. For portraits of both men by a writer who was familiar with their lives and work
see Robert Duffus, "Jacques Loeb: Mechanist," *Century Magazine*, 108 (1924): 374-
83, and *The Innocents at Cedro* (New York: Macmillian, 1944).

have been instrumental in getting Veblen a position in the economics department at Stanford. More importantly, however, their correspondence and use of each other's ideas are significant both in understanding the simultaneous evolution of their own thought and Loeb's influence on the development of Veblen's theory of instincts.

Veblen and Loeb shared a common radical political outlook and convergent research objectives, as unusual as this may seem for an economist and a biologist; both attempted to undermine theories that rested on unscientific or, more often, prescientific, that is, pre-Darwinian grounds.[2] Both aimed at discrediting vitalistic, teleological, introspective, animistic, anthropomorphic, metaphysical and spiritualistic explanations of both the natural and social order.[3] Loeb was most aggressive in his attempts to establish the general principles of an antimetaphysical science of physiology, while Veblen attacked the scientific pretensions and status of neoclassical economics and advocated its replacement with a genuinely evolutionary approach. They thus represented the vanguard of the Darwinian movement in the United States in the

2. Loeb's dislike of efforts to explain human behavior on non-scientific grounds is evident throughout his correspondence. For example, on 11 September 1920 he wrote to the American novelist Theodore Dreiser that:

> No exact work has been done on human behavior. The psychiatrists, of course, have to deal with the subject but their work is more or less of an amateurish character. Twenty-five years ago hysteria was a la mode under the influence and leadership of Charcot in Paris, then an era of hypnotism followed, and now we have the wave of Freudianism. While in all of these hypotheses there is some basis of fact, the methods are so amateurish and crude that nothing permanent has or can come of it. Unless we can get exact methods such as I have tried to introduce in the form of the tropism theory in lower animals, we have to be satisfied with admitting our ignorance.

On 26 February 1920 he wrote to the psychologist Joseph Jastrow, who was conducting a study of belief among scientists in extranatural and parapsychic phenomena, to state that "needless to say, I neither believe in spirits nor in telepathy." Earlier, and perhaps most tellingly, he had written to Joseph McCabe on 18 December 1919 that "if our *life is simply,* as I think I have shown, *the time required to complete a single or a series of chemical reactions,* [author's emphasis] one does not quite understand what sense there is left for an assumption of life after death—Is such a life also the time required for the "spirit" to complete a series of chemical reactions and how does the temperature affect it?"

3. Loeb's dislike of Bergson's vitalism and its influence in the United States caused him to write that: "I take pleasure in sending you a pamphlet which I wrote two years ago, chiefly to counteract the epidemic of Bergsonism among the cultivated Americans," Loeb to Joseph McCabe, 9 April 1918. On 22 December 1921 he wrote to McCabe that "I shall send you an article published recently in the Revue Philosophique . . . it might make Brother Bergson jump. When he was in America he denounced me as a very dangerous man."

natural and social sciences respectively.[4]

It is known from Loeb's and Veblen's correspondence and Veblen's citations that the latter read Loeb's *Heliotropismus der Thiere* (1889) *Comparative Physiology of the Brain and Comparative Psychology* (1900), *The Dynamics of Living Matter* (1906), *The Mechanistic Conception of Life* (1912), and *Forced Movements, Tropisms and Animal Conduct* (1918). It is also known that Loeb read several of Veblen's books upon which he commented in letters.[5] It is Loeb's influence on Veblen and the convergence in their thinking, however, particularly as it pertains to instincts, that is the focus of this analysis.

Both Loeb and Veblen devoted much of their serious work as scientists and scholars to attacking teleological constructs and influences; Loeb in his physiological research and experimentation attempted to undermine teleomechanistic claims regarding the behavior of organisms; Veblen, in developing his institutionalist critique of neoclassical economics, castigated the classicals and neoclassicals for attributing goal-oriented or purposive aims to fluctuations of supply and demand in markets. It was not surprising that both would detect and expose teleology when it was embedded by animists in the natural order or by the eminent French philosopher Henri Bergson in the cosmic order.

Did Veblen share Loeb's belief that the truth of mechanistic materialism could be demonstrated by uncovering the physical and chemical bases of biological phenomena? It is impossible to say with any degree of certainty; Veblen was intrigued by such possibilities yet he was not well grounded in physics or chemistry and, in any case, was too much influenced by both the skepticism of David Hume and the idealism of Immanuel Kant to subscribe dogmatically to reductionism. Loeb believed that perception and behavior were largely biological functions, while Veblen was more open to the view that the social and cultural environment induces a wide variety of reactions on the part of humankind. It appears, however, that there was no real conflict in their outlooks only a matter of emphasis on

---

4. Unlike some of his contemporaries, however, Loeb was critical of Darwinians and Darwinism because he regarded evolutionary theory as the beginning not the end of scientific inquiry. For example, on 4 October 1916 he wrote to the English biologist Julian Huxley that:

> In thinking over your remark about my statement concerning the theory of natural selection in the Preface of my book which you were good enough to read I made a change which I think will be satisfactory to you. It now reads, "The theory of natural selection invokes neither design nor purpose, but it is incomplete since it disregards the physical-chemical constitution of living matter about which little was known until recently."

5. See esp. Veblen to Loeb, 20 February 1913 and Loeb to Veblen, 3 January 1919.

institutional as opposed to physiological factors.

Economists have attempted to understand better Veblen's use of psychology and biology; from this they hoped to deduce a more effective explanation of his methodological strictures and usages.[6] Often, they have tried to accomplish this by examining his intellectual pedigree and have relied heavily on Joseph Dorfman's *Thorstein Veblen and His America* (1934) to interpret the various influences on him. It is our contention, however, that Loeb's impact on Veblen was greater than is commonly supposed and, perhaps more important, that the convergence in their thinking reveals much about Veblen's own use of concepts drawn from psychology and biology.

It is worth noting that, in the past, those alleging the influence of Loeb on Veblen have often made their claims without textual exegesis of Loeb's work and without examining the correspondence between the two men. It can be shown that not only did Loeb influence Veblen, but that the vagueness and inconsistency in Veblen's theory of instincts can be traced, in part, to problems which arose in Loeb's own work in mechanistic physiology. The meaning of Veblen's theory of instincts, and the confusion which has arisen among Veblen scholars in interpreting it, was caused in part by Loeb's own difficulties in distinguishing between tropisms, reflexes and instincts.[7] This may be a reflection of the difficulty Loeb had in demonstrating the relationship between his own brilliant laboratory experiments on lower forms of animal life and the nature and behavior of human beings. Loeb could not adequately explain the formation of ideational patterns in the brain of Homo sapiens through his own experiments or those of others[8] but he believed that, at least in principle, the cerebral processes that produced

---

6. Cf. esp. A. W. Coats, "The Influence of Veblen's Methodology," *Journal of Political Economy*, 62 (Dec., 1954): 529-37, Lev E. Dobriansky, *Veblenism: A New Critique* (Washington, D.C.: Public Affairs Press, 1957) Chaps. 4, 5, 6.

7. Some light is shed on Loeb's problems in distinguishing between instincts, reflexes and tropisms in his correspondence with the behaviorist John B. Watson. On 3 January 1914 Loeb wrote to Watson that:

> I do not think there is any fault to be found in the "reflex," not much is meant, while in the case of tropism we deal with metrical quantities and I do not know that this is the conditio sine qua non. That is the reason also that I do not think the theory of "trial and error" can lead to measurable quantities in science. The idea of tropisms works quite well if we proceed, as the physicist does, with eliminating the disturbance variables.

8. "Thus far we have not touched upon the most important problem in physiology namely, which mechanisms give rise to that complex of phenomena which are called psychic or conscious. Our method of procedure must be the same as in the

thought would eventually be explained by physical chemistry. What Veblen thought about this is unknown, but it is evident that he used Loeb's other concepts and the empirical findings on which they rested and this became one source of the difficulties found in his theory of instincts.

It is interesting to note that in one very significant passage in *Comparative Physiology of the Brain and Comparative Psychology* (1900), Loeb uses Veblen's "instinct of workmanship" as both an analytical device and a normative prescription, and in a footnote specifically attributes this concept to him.[9] This footnote provides evidence exclusive of their correspondence that Loeb thought Veblen understood him properly since he used a concept of indisputably Veblenian origin in his own work.[10]

Loeb did not claim that he or any other scientist had yet discovered an adequate explanation of mental processes, but he was willing to propose that the simple reactions thus far observed in lower organisms would provide the beginning of an understanding of the more complex processes observable in higher organisms. He argued that the underlying processes at the level of physical chemistry are the same in both higher and lower organisms; however the number and complexity of underlying simple reactions are far different. He suggested that a number of tropismatic reactions in lower animals were understood and that when these results come to be greatly multiplied they "will show the addition necessary to the tropismatic theory to make it include the endless number of reactions in which associative memory is involved."[11]

Loeb's research agenda, which he never completed, ultimately

---

case of instincts and reflexes. We must find out the elementary physiological processes which underlie the complicated phenomena of consciousness." Loeb, *Comparative Physiology of the Brain and Comparative Psychology*, (New York: G. P. Putnam's Sons, 1900) p. 10.

9. Ibid., p. 197.

10. Unlike some natural scientists, Loeb was neither ignorant nor naive about political affairs. His views were roughly convergent with Veblen's and he occasionally mentioned the latter in his correspondence. This was particularly true during the First World War when he often echoed Veblen's sentiments on Imperial Germany. To illustrate, he wrote to his son Leonard on 8 June 1917: "I think Veblen is right, the German Government has to cease to exist, otherwise neither this generation nor the next will know any peace; with the collapse of the German autocracy that of the Japanese will collapse too, because they are simply imitating." Three days later, he wrote to Leonard that "as far as the Germans are concerned, there is absolutely no question that Veblen is right and that unless that government is driven to the wall the world will see no peace."

11. Ibid., p. 171.

rested on his belief that mental processes might best be understood through progress in physical chemistry.[12] To what extent did Loeb think that his own research agenda had been realized? In his publications which it is likely Veblen read, Loeb makes no sweeping or definitive claims. We do get progress reports, however, such as his 1912 discussion, found in *The Mechanistic Conception of Life*. He expressed satisfaction that for a few clearly identified animal behaviors, experimental results were able to provide complete explanations based on physical chemistry; furthermore these behaviors were of the nature of "phenomena which the metaphysician would classify under the term of animal 'will'." He found this degree of progress far from satisfactory, however. "A mechanistic conception of life is not complete unless it includes a physico-chemical explanation of psychic phenomena." (Of course, by "psychic" Loeb was making reference to mental processes, not communication with the supernatural world!) He even acknowledged that many prominent scientists argued that the "truly psychical" would never be explained on the basis of physical chemistry, but Loeb was convinced to the contrary. He concluded, however, that since that goal was far off and so much work remained to be done at a lower level, such a debate was premature.[13]

Veblen's and Loeb's mockery of teleologism, vitalism, traditional metaphysics, spiritualism, anthropomorphism and other

---

12. See Loeb, *Comparative Physiology of the Brain and Comparative Psychology*, p. 214.

13. Loeb, *The Mechanistic Conception of Life*, p. 35. Perhaps the most direct application of Loebian doctrine to Veblen's analysis of public policy is his satirical comment that:

> It appears always to be a matter of "forced movements" rather than an outcome of shrewd initiative and logical design—even though much argument may be spent in the course of it all. As witness the helplessly evil case of the civilized nations since the War and the Armistice, and the solicitous fluttering of all the shrewd statesmen and the responsible men of affairs. When seen in a longer historical perspective and with a consequent greater detachment of observation any deliberate revision of the received scheme of law and morals will appear all the more patently to be a work of casual drift and an outcome of fortuitous habituation—Forced Movements, Tropisms, and Animal Conduct. Such in effect has been a growth of nationalism in recent times, as well as of the progressively expanded rights of absentee ownership during the same period.

In two footnotes on the same page Veblen comments that:

> The form of words made use of above will be recognized as taken from the title of a volume published by Jacques Loeb under the caption. In all this it remains true, of course, that interested parties have shrewdly turned these forced movements of popular sentiment of account, and so have exercised something of a selective guidance over the growth of institutions.

Veblen, *Absentee Ownership*, (Boston: Beacon Press, 1967) pp. 19-20.

such intellectual tendencies is exemplified in this quotation from Veblen which specifically focuses on anthropomorphic portrayals of animal behavior:

> Even more to the same purpose, as shown the same insidious facility of anthropomorphic interpretation, are the bona-fide constructions of scientists and pseudo-scientists running on the imputation of purpose and deliberation to explain the behavior of animals. Indeed, at the worst, and still in good faith, it may go so far as to impute some sort of quasi-conscious striving on the part of plants. As good and temperate an instance as may be had of such anthropomorphic imputation of workman-like gifts is afforded, for instance, by the work of Romanes on the behavior of animals. It goes to show how very plausibly some of the lower animals may be credited with these spiritual aptitudes and how far and well the imputation may be made to serve the scientist's end.[14]

Although Veblen did not often comment extensively on Loeb's work in his own writings, his and Loeb's epistemological and metatheoretical covergence made them easily recognizable as products of the same cultural and intellectual milieu and, importantly, as sharing similar political and moral values. The convergence in Loeb's and Veblen's research agenda did not bring the latter into the research laboratory as an experimental physiologist. It did, however, bring him within doctrinal proximity of this Loeb statement regarding the prospects of a better understanding of the human condition:

> The contents of life from the cradle to the bier are wishes and hopes, efforts and struggles, and unfortunately also disappointments and suffering. And this inner life should be amenable to a physico-chemical analysis? In spite of the gulf which separates us today from such an aim I believe that it is attainable. As long as a life phenomenon has not yet found a physico-chemical explanation it usually appears inexplicable. If the veil is once lifted we are always surprised that we did not guess from the first what was behind it. That in the case of our inner life a physico-chemical explanation is not beyond the realm of possibility is proved by the fact that it is already possible for us to explain cases of simple manifestations of animal instinct and will on a physico-chemical basis; namely, the phenomena which I have discussed in former papers under the name of animal tropisms.[15]

---

14. Veblen, *The Instinct of Workmanship*, pp. 75-6.

15. Ibid., p. 26.

Part of what Veblen and Loeb had in common may be described as a predisposition on the part of the former toward "social control" in political economy and on the part of the latter to favor the "engineering ideal" in biology.[16] For Veblen, this implied regulation of economic affairs while, for Loeb, it led him to comment that "the aim of modern biology is no longer word discussions, but the control of life-phenomena."[17] Loeb's and Veblen's epistemological and metatheoretical commonalities thus led them not only to the formulation of a convergent research agenda, but also to a common set of moral and social ideals which still seek a vehicle for their political realization.

In their common resistance to metaphysical, spiritualistic, vitalistic and anthropomorphic explanations in the natural and social sciences, respectively, both Loeb and Veblen turned to deterministic explanations based on instincts, tropisms and reflexes.[18] Loeb contended that the phenomena, in turn, were products of physico-chemical events which could be explained in a purely mechanistic fashion. Not being a partner in the laboratories of the natural sciences, Veblen drew upon the work of Loeb and other scientists of the day in developing his own conceptualization of instincts, tropisms and reflexes and their explanatory utility in understanding human behavior. It was thus inevitable that definitional weaknesses and inconsistencies in the natural sciences should appear, or even become amplified, in his social scientific work.

Phillip Pauly commented to this effect on Loeb's role at Chicago: "He . . . was one of the few supporters of Thorstein Veblen, though he told his son he thought 'Veblen's inclinations were a bit screwball'."[19] In a footnote Pauly continues: "The only element of Veblen's thought that Loeb took seriously was his 'instinct of

16. See Rick Tilman, *Thorstein Veblen and His Critics, 1891-1963: Conservative, Liberal and Radical Perspectives* (Princeton: Princeton University Press, 1992) and Phillip J. Pauly, *Controlling Life: Jacques Loeb and the Engineering Ideal in Biology* (New York: Oxford University Press, 1987).

17. Loeb, *Comparative Physiology of the Brain and Comparative Psychology*, p. 287.

18. This impersonal character of intelligence is, of course, most evident on the lower levels of life. If we follow Mr. Loeb, e.g., in his inquiries into the psychology of the life that lies below the threshold of intelligence, what we meet with is an aimless but unwavering motor response to stimulus.
Veblen, *The Place of Science in Modern Civilization*, (New York: Viking Press, 1930) pp. 5-6.

19. As quoted in Philip J. Pauly, *Controlling Life: Jacques Loeb and the Engineering Ideal in Biology*, p. 71.

workmanship'—the drive to make things and make them well; this was in large part an Americanization of Popper-Lynkeus's 'engineering impulse'."[20] Progressive evolutionism was an important part of Loeb's and Veblen's intellectual milieu, yet they reacted to it differently than did their Chicago colleagues. Indeed, Loeb became a radical opponent of the evolutionary foundations on which Chicago Progressivism was built for, as Pauly has argued," his vision of biology as engineering and his practice of experimentation made the human future disturbingly open-ended."[21] The extent to which Veblen agreed with Loeb's reductionistic epistemology and mechanistic materialist ontology is an open question, but he certainly shared Loeb's view that the outcome of the evolutionary process might not be a happy one. As Henry Steele Commager stated many years ago, "While others saw progress, Veblen saw only change."[22] The Chicago faculty, with varying degrees of explicitness, linked their evolutionary ideas to belief in the probability of human progress, but this optimism was not shared by either of our two central figures.

LOEB'S MECHANISTIC PHYSIOLOGY

Loeb was noted for his mechanistic physiology which led him to the conclusion that "life, i.e., the sum of all life phenomena, can be unequivocally explained in physico-chemical terms."[23] He took as a first principle that "our existence is based on the play of blind forces, and [is] only a matter of chance . . . we ourselves are only chemical mechanisms."[24] With biological changes strongly established in the quantitative terms of physics and chemistry and with human behavior a predictable response to chemical tropisms, what

---

20. Ibid., p. 214. N. Pauly is referring to the following passage, "One of the most important instincts is usually not even recognized as such namely, the instinct of workmanship . . . I take this name from Veblen's book *The Theory of the Leisure Class.*" Cf. Loeb, *Comparative Physiology of the Brain and Comparative Psychology* (New York: Arno Press, 1973) p. 197, 233. Also, cf. Loeb, *The Mechanistic Conception of Life* (Chicago: University of Chicago Press, 1912) pp. 30, 31, and Duffus "Jacques Loeb: Mechanist," p. 380.

21. Pauly, *Controlling Life*, p. 7.

22. Henry Steele Commager, *The American Mind* (New Haven: Yale University Press, 1950) p. 239.

23. Loeb, *The Mechanistic Conception of Life*, p. 3.

24. Ibid., p. 31.

remained to be explained was the role of values in the world of fact:

> How can there be an ethics for us? The answer is, that our
> instincts are the root of our ethics and that the instincts are just
> as hereditary as is the form of our body. We eat, drink and
> reproduce not because mankind has reached an agreement
> that this is desirable, but because, machine-like, we are
> compelled to do so . . . we struggle for justice and truth since
> we are instinctively compelled to see our fellow beings happy.[25]

To Veblen effective ethical norms are those that aid in the
instrumentally adaptive efforts of the community to adjust to
environmental change and they are not so much value constant
instinctual forms of behavior as they are learned. In short, morality
is not simply epiphenomenal excretion from hereditary traits, but a
response to the evolutionary constraints placed on humankind by
nature and society. That Loeb was committed to a conception of life
similar to Veblen's is likely as this quotation indicates:

> Economic, social and political conditions or ignorance and
> superstition may warp and inhibit the inherited instincts and
> thus create a civilization with a low development of ethics.
> Individual mutants may arise in which one or other desirable
> instinct is lost, just as individual mutants without pigment may
> arise in animals; and the offsprings of such mutants may, if
> numerous enough, lower the ethical status of a community . . .
> not only is the mechanistic conception of life compatible with
> ethics; it seems the only conception of life which can lead to an
> understanding of the source of ethics.[26]

Nevertheless, like Veblen, particularly in his later works such as
The Instinct of Workmanship (1914), and *Imperial Germany and the
Industrial Revolution* (1915), Loeb sought to discredit racialist
arguments especially when they were used to arouse jingoism and
promote war and imperialism. Loeb's public responses to the War
constitute some of the more radical formulations of opposition to
the fighting on the Western Front. He said the war made him
"literally sick,"[27] and he framed a heated plea against the jingoism
of the time in "Biology and War."

In this latter discussion, Loeb states that the war being waged in

---

25. As quoted in Gerald Weissman (foreword by Lewis Thomas), *The Woods Hole
Cantata: Essays on Science and Society*, (New York: Raven, 1985), p. 6.

26. Loeb, *The Mechanistic Conception of Life*, p. 31.

27. Duffus, "Jacques Loeb: Mechanist," p. 380.

Europe would be impossible without the support of a broad spectrum of the citizens of each of the nations involved "for wars are impossible unless the masses are aroused to a state of emotionalism and fanaticism." He argues that the underpinning of this massive war fever is the perception by national groups of their own inherited superiority and, as a corollary, the inherent inferiority of their opponents in the conflict. This system of beliefs in a biologically based superiority versus inferiority of national group was instilled in the masses, Loeb believed, by "quotations from the erudite statements of theologians, philologists, historians, politicians, anthropologists, and also occasionally of biologists, especially of the nonexperimental type."

Once again, it may be noted, Loeb ranks religious leaders high on the list of contributors to social problems, including war. Loeb was particularly upset by the contributions biology and the "pseudobiology of litterateurs . . ." to the developing concept of "racial biology" which attempts to justify—or even require in a moral sense the subjugation of inferior ethnic groups by superior ethnic (national) groups, or "superior races" and "inferior races" in Loeb's words. Who decides "inferior" or "superior"? Loeb answered that "the relative values of races is furnished by a group of writers who call themselves 'racial biologists'." He argued that this "pseudobiology" was based on outdated, antiquated and speculative notions of biology, that there was no basis of support for its claims in a mechanistic approach to life phenomena and that this "pseudobiology" was in no way based on experimental results. In light of more advanced concepts of biology based on the principles of physical chemistry, a biological basis for justifying the War evaporated.[28]

The racial biology to which Loeb refers was part of the intellectual environment in the late nineteenth and early twentieth centuries; scholars in many disciplines had to come to terms with it, and Veblen himself was no exception to the rule. The biogenetic determinism that linked psychological type to racial or ethnic stock was widespread and Veblen was middle-aged before he largely jettisoned it. It appears that Loeb was a leading influence in helping him to do so.

VEBLEN, LOEB AND THE INSTINCT THEORY

Veblen scholars have differed significantly over the source of his ideas regarding human behavior, particularly their roots in physiological psychology. William James, William McDougall, Charles Darwin, C.

---

28. Loeb, "Biology and War," *Science*, (26 January 1917): 74-5.

Lloyd Morgan and Jacques Loeb, or some combination thereof, have received nomination from Veblen scholars as primary influences on him. It is also commonplace to attribute his ideas about instinctual behavior to Veblen's reading of four authors whose work is generally regarded as seminal in the genesis of his theory.[29] These authors are James, particularly his *Principles of Psychology*, Loeb, especially his *Comparative Physiology of the Brain and Comparative Psychology*, Morgan *Habit and Instinct and Introduction to Comparative Psychology*, and McDougall *Introduction to Social Psychology*. Veblen cites these authors repeatedly in *The Instinct of Workmanship*, the first portion of which contains his most complete and consistent analysis of the meaning of "tropisms" and "instincts."[30] Whatever the case may be in terms of the primacy and magnitude of these influences, it is easier to document and explain the influence of Loeb on Veblen because much of the correspondence between the two men is in the Loeb papers in the Library of Congress.

Veblen divided what he called human "instincts" into two categories, the peaceful and the predatory. The peaceful instincts were those of workmanship, parenthood and idle curiosity; the predatory instincts were the pecuniary and sporting. Veblen believed that these traits had appeared in both prehistory and in historical times in both pure and mixed (contaminated) forms. Even the casual reader of *The Theory of the Leisure Class* (1899), where the instinct theory is most fully utilized and explicated, will recognize Veblen's preference for the peaceful as opposed to the predatory type. However, as Veblen scholars have noted, his employment of the concept is not merely analytical, it is also prescriptive and normative for he attempts to both explain and evaluate. He thus aims at understanding not only the relationship between peaceful and predatory traits in particular societies, but the role of these traits in increasing or diminishing continuity of life and re-creation of noninvidious community.[31]

Veblen's use of the term "instinct" is a case of a vocabulary in transition which perhaps explains his ambiguous and occasionally inconsistent utilization of it. At times, he is undecided as to whether instincts are innate, learned or both. However, he exhibits considerable sensitivity to the problem with his distinction between

29. See Footnote 10 in this regard.

30. See Veblen, *The Instinct of Workmanship* (New York: B. W. Huebsch, 1918), Chap. 1.

31. See Marc Tool, *Essays in Social Value Theory* (Armonk, N.Y.: M. E. Sharpe, 1986) pp. 56-61.

"tropisms," which he defined as forms of innate behavior present in the species at birth, and "instincts" which he considered to be learned behavior become habitual through institutional conditioning.[32] His sensitivity toward the difference between tropismatic and learned behavior is most evident in his later work and undoubtedly owes much to his reading of Loeb's work and to conversations with him.

From Loeb's standpoint, the most important and general quality of reflexes was their regularity. On the basis of his redefinition of the reflex in purely functional terms, he was able to argue that tropisms and instincts were complex combinations of reflexes.[33] This aspect of Loeb's work influenced Veblen's understanding of physiological psychology, but he, in turn, also influenced Loeb as the following quotation clearly shows:

> [Loeb] argued . . . that ethics were expressions of instincts such as motherhood, workmanship, and the desire to see one's neighbor happy; these instincts, he concluded, were "chemically and hereditarily fixed in us in the same definite fashion as the shapes of our bodies."[34]

Two of these "instincts" are, of course, identical with those utilized by Veblen throughout his writing, namely, the parental bent and the instinct of workmanship. A third, "idle curiosity," Loeb does not mention.

INSTINCTS, REFLEXES AND TROPISMS: THE SOURCE OF CONFUSION

Veblen referred to the concept of instinct as a "shifty" notion and once confessed to Clarence Ayres that "he had never clearly defined it."[35] However, it is evident in two of his most important books *The*

---

32. See Veblen, *The Instinct of Workmanship*, Chap. 1.

33. See Pauly, *Controlling Life*, p. 122.

34. Ibid., p. 140.

35. Veblen's own ambiguity toward the meaning of the term "instinct" is evident in a conversation that took place in his home between him and Clarence Ayres in the spring of 1920. Ayres reported that:
It was on this occasion that a conversational exchange occurred which I have often repeated to students apropos V's [Veblen's] conception of "instincts." He asked me point blank if I recalled exactly how he had defined instincts. I was flabbergasted, and after a long moment's soul-searching I replied that I couldn't recall any exact definition. He beamed, and said, "No, you can't, because I never did!"
Clarence Ayres to Louis Junker, 18 July 1966, Clarence E. Ayres Papers, Center for American History, University of Texas Austin.

Theory of the Leisure Class (1899), and *The Instinct of Workmanship* (1914), that it plays an important role in his social theory. In the past, critics have complained with justice that his use of "instinct" in his early work is ambiguous, even contradictory, and that he fails to adequately differentiate between instincts, tropisms and reflexes.[36] However, our focus here is to explain how and why Loeb's writings on mechanistic physiology may be one source of Veblen's problems. Also, it will be argued that by 1914 Veblen had partly overcome several of these problems and was using "tropisms," "reflexes" and "instincts" in a clearer and more conceptually consistent fashion.

Loeb distinguished conceptually between tropisms, reflexes and instincts. In the five books he wrote that Veblen read he argued that tropisms were forced movements involving the organism as a whole and were induced by physico-chemical processes interacting with the organism's environment. They were not purposive acts "willed" by the organism be it plant or animal, but simply the consequences of its inherited structural properties. Loeb performed experiments to demonstrate tropismatic reactions caused by contact with electricity, light, chemicals and solid surfaces. However, in Veblen's eyes most socially significant human behavior is not merely tropismatic—it is reflexive and, more important, it is also instinctual. It is, therefore, necessary to compare what Loeb wrote on these subjects with what Veblen wrote. In 1912 in *The Mechanistic Conception of Life* Loeb stated that:

> While some authors explain all reflexes on a psychical basis, the majority of investigators explain in this way only a certain group of reflexes—the so-called instincts. Instincts are defined in various ways, but no matter how the definition is phrased the meaning seems to be that they are inherited reflexes so

---

36. Veblen scholars disagree over the sources of Veblen's ideas regarding human nature and behavior. For example, David Riesman, *Thorstein Veblen: A Critical Interpretation* (New York: Charles Scribner's Sons, 1960) stresses the influence of James on pp. 19, 25, 40, 58, 79n, 120; McDougall, p. 54; Loeb, pp. 19, 54, 205. John P. Diggins, *The Bard of Savagery: Thorstein Veblen and Modern Social Theory* (New York: The Seabury Press, 1978) emphasizes the influence of James and Loeb; see pp. 4, 37, 182, 222, 229; Allan G. Gruchy, *Modern Economic Thought: The American Contribution* (New York: Prentice-Hall, 1947) focuses on James on pp. 62-3, 254-55. Wesley C. Mitchell (ed.), *What Veblen Taught* (New York: Augustus M. Kelley, 1964) xxx-xxxiv stresses the influence of James, Darwin and Loeb; Joseph Dorfman, *Thorstein Veblen and His America* (New York: Viking Press, 1934) emphasizes the influence of James on p. 450 and Loeb on pp. 115, 196, 277. Although he does not claim Morgan had a direct influence on Veblen, he mentions Morgan's contribution to the existing intellectual milieu on pp. 115, 139. Bernard Rosenberg, (ed.), *Thorstein Veblen* (New York: Thomas Y. Crowell, 1963) emphasizes Loeb, Darwin, and James on p. 2. John R. Commons in his *Institutional*

purposeful and so complicated in character that nothing short
of intelligence and experience could have produced them.[37]

However, Loeb believed that there was no sharp line of
demarcation between reflexes and instincts. He, in fact, noted that
authors preferred to "speak of reflexes in cases where the reaction
of single parts or organs of an animal to external stimuli is
concerned; while they speak of instincts where the reaction of the
animal as a whole is involved (as is the case in tropisms)."[38] To make
matters still more complex, he also wrote that:

> . . . the theory of tropisms is at the same time the theory of
> instincts if due consideration is given to the role of hormones in
> producing certain tropisms and suppressing others. A systematic
> analysis of instinctive reactions from the viewpoint of the theory
> of tropisms and hormones will probably yield rich returns.[39]

Because of the complexity of Loeb's writings and his occasional
inconsistencies, it is not surprising that Veblen's own writings
should reveal similar deficiencies. The conceptual crudities and
ambiguity of his otherwise brilliant *The Theory of the Leisure Class*
(1899), gave way to the more informed and definitive tones of *The
Instinct of Workmanship* (1914), where more precise differentiation is
made between tropisms and instincts. In this latter work, Veblen
argues that instinctive behaviors are nevertheless subject to
"modification by habit." Here he further states that behaviors which
are not subject to adaptation through repetition should not be
labeled "instincts," but should "rather be classed as tropismatic."
Thus Veblen states that instincts, particularly in humans, are a class
of behaviors in which only "the end of endeavour" is determined,
while the means to that end are open to "reflection, discretion and
deliberate adaptation."[40] In clarification of the meaning of instinct

Economics, Vol. II, (Madison: University of Wisconsin Press, 1961) p. 661, stresses
the influence of Darwin. C. E. Ayres, "Veblen Theory of Instincts" in Douglas
Dowd, (ed.) *Thorstein Veblen: A Critical Reappraisal* (Ithaca, N.Y.: Cornell University
Press, 1958) emphasizes the intellectual milieu influenced by James and
McDougall on p. 28. Lev Dobriansky, *Veblenism: A New Critique*, (Washington, D.C.
Public Affairs Press, 1957) stresses the influence of Loeb, McDougall, and James on
pp. 17, 121, 170, 250, 253, 257.

37. Loeb, *The Mechanistic Conception of Life*, pp. 68-9.

38. Loeb, *Comparative Physiology of the Brain and Comparative Psychology*, pp. 7-8.

39. Loeb, *Forced Movements, Tropisms and Animal Conduct*, p. 163.

40. Veblen, *The Instinct of Workmanship*, p. 38.

Veblen also writes:

> All instinctive action is intelligent and teleological. The generality of instinctive dispositions point simply to the direct and unambiguous attainment of their specific ends . . . the agent goes as directly as may be to the end sought,—he is occupied with the objective end, not with the choice of means to the end sought; whereas under the impulse of workmanship the agent's interest and endeavour are taken up with the contriving of ways and means to the end sought.[41]

Prior to this, Veblen, on many occasions, had specifically referred to the "instinct of workmanship"; now it is interesting to note that he has relabeled it the "impulse" of workmanship. Is this again evidence of his vague, at times contradictory, conceptualization of instincts? In any case, he now states that instincts are aimed at the attainment of ends, but the impulse of workmanship aims at the "contriving of ways and means to the end sought."[42]

In principle there may be no reason why "instincts" as such could not be oriented toward the achievement of either ends or means, yet, again, this does suggest an ambiguity in the concept itself. However, even in one of his most conceptually lucid statements Veblen wrote that:

> In making use of the expression, "instinct of workmanship" or "sense of workmanship," it is not here intended to assume or to argue that the proclivity so designated is in the psychological respect a simple or irreducible element; still less, of course, is there any intention to allege that it is to be traced back in the physiological respect to some one isolatable tropismatic sensibility or some single enzymatic or visceral stimulus. All that is matter for the attention of those whom it may concern. The expression may as well be taken to signify a concurrence of several instinctive aptitudes, each of which might or might not prove simple or irreducible when subjected to psychological or physiological analysis. For the present inquiry it is enough to note that in human behavior this disposition is effective in such consistent, ubiquitous and resilient fashion that students of human culture will have to count with it as one of the integral hereditary traits of mankind.[43]

---

41. Ibid., p. 32.

42. Ibid., p. 27.

43. Ibid., pp. 27-8.

Veblen also argues against the position taken by his Missouri colleague Maurice Parmalee in *The Science of Human Behavior* (1913). Parmalee had claimed that since "instinct" was not a neurological or physiological concept, it could not be stated in neurological or physiological terms. Veblen was critical of Parmalee for wanting to dispense with the concept of "instinct" because he, Veblen, saw great value in the concept of instinct as an explanatory tool in attempting mechanistic explanations of psychological phenomena. He took pains to make clear that he was in no way attempting to supplant psychological terms with mechanistic alternatives, but rather to use the latter as a means of conceptualizing the former, and he cites Loeb's *Comparative Physiology of the Brain and Comparative Psychology* in doing so.[44] Loeb's mechanism is, of course, discussed elsewhere in this book in some detail so we shall not discuss it any further here except to suggest that whatever reservations Veblen may have harbored about it are rarely expressed in his writing.

The ambiguity, vagueness and, at times, contradictions found in Loeb's use of "instinct" can also be found in Veblen's published work. Take, for example, the following quotation from *The Instinct of Workmanship* (1914) which is most illustrative of Veblen's problem:

> The instincts, all and several, though perhaps in varying degrees, are so intimately engaged in a play of give and take that the work of any one has its consequences for all the rest, though presumably not for all equally. It is this endless complication and contamination of instinctive elements in human conduct, taken in conjunction with the pervading and cumulative effects of habit in this domain, that makes most of the difficulty and much of the interest attaching to this line of inquiry.[45]

To which Veblen adds in a footnote, "Endless in the sense that the effects of such concatenation do not run to a final term in any direction."[46] Another telling example of the same problem in Veblen follows the first:

> There are few lines of instinctive proclivity that are not crossed and colored by some ramification of the instinct of workmanship. No doubt, response to the direct call of such half-tropismatic, half-instinctive impulses as hunger, anger, or the

---

44. Ibid., p. 28.

45. Ibid., p. 29.

46. Ibid.

prompting of sex, is little if at all troubled with any sentimental suffusion of workmanship; but in the more complex and deliberate activities, particularly when habit exerts an appreciable effect, the impulse and sentiment of workmanship comes in for a large share in the outcome. So much so, indeed, that, for instance, in the arts, where the sense of beauty is the prime mover, habitual attention to technique will often put the original, and only ostensible, motive in the background.[47]

Veblen clearly reveals the conceptual inadequacy of his own instinct theory with his phrase "such half-tropismatic, half-instinctive impulses as hunger, anger, or the prompting of sex." He is unable at this point to make any clear-cut distinction between tropisms and instincts and so finds both in impulses such as hunger, anger and sex. Despite Veblen's valiant and partially successful efforts to come to grips with the new findings in physiological psychology, efforts that few if any other contemporary economists made, he ultimately fails for lack of conceptual precision.

The problem can be further illustrated with reference to Veblen's own inconsistency as to whether his "instincts" are themselves means or ends. He is, however, consistent in his claim that instincts as he defines them are purposive rather than anarchic or random in their expression.

But like other innate predispositions the parental bent continually reasserts itself in its native and untaught character, as an ever resilient solicitude for the welfare of the young and the prospective fortunes of the group. As such it constantly comes in to reenforce the instinct of workmanship and sustain interest in the direct pursuit of efficiency in the ways and means of life. So closely in touch and so concurrent are the parental bent and the sense of workmanship in this quest of efficiency that it is commonly difficult to guess which of the two proclivities is to be credited with the larger or the leading part in any given line of conduct; although taken by and large the two are after all fairly distinct in respect of their functional content. This thorough and far-going concurrence of the two may perhaps be taken to mean that the instinct of workmanship is in the main a propensity to work out the ends which the parental bent makes worth while.[48]

An important qualification of the conditions under which instincts may manifest themselves lends more precise meaning to the concept of instinct itself. For example, in *The Instinct of*

---

47. Ibid.

48. Ibid., p. 48.

Workmanship, Veblen cites idle curiosity as one of a group of instincts which "constitutes the spiritual predispositions of man," and as such comes into force or operation only after more immediate demands such as "nutrition, growth and reproduction" have been satisfied. He further states that the expression of the instinct of idle curiosity is constrained by the energy that remains after more immediate needs have been met, that is "within the bounds of that metabolic margin of surplus energy," to use Veblen's expression.[49]

It is likely that Veblen also believed that the other instincts in his taxonomy would likewise be affected by the need to satisfy metabolic needs. The flowering of the instincts was thus dependent on both the satisfaction of basic biological needs *and* the proper set of institutional arrangements. Again, however, these qualifications, important though they be, contribute only modestly to solving the problem of conceptual clarity in Veblen's work.

POLITICS, WALL STREET AND WAR

The outbreak of war in the summer of 1914 greatly affected both Veblen and Loeb. It prompted Veblen to finish quickly and publish *Imperial Germany and the Industrial Revolution,* a copy of which he sent to Loeb. After reading parts of it, Loeb commented on 16 August 1915 that:

> Needless to say that the war has shattered all my ideals and hopes. . . . The profits which certain bankers and armament manufacturers in this country are making at present makes it very obvious that our days of a peaceful nation are numbered. Our businessmen will . . . make trouble in other countries and thus stir up war. . . . The other day I heard the story that when Wilson's administration came in, Pierpont Morgan, who was negotiating a loan with China, sent one of his representatives to Wilson to inquire whether he will stand by the promise given to him by the previous administration of letting them have the use of the American Army and Navy if necessary. When this was refused, the loan fell through. If this country should have gone to war with China, our historians, journalists, and other patriots would have given the whole glory to the generals and the diplomats, while modest Mr. Morgan would have been satisfied with the cash and otherwise kept in the background.[50]

---

49. Ibid., p. 86.

50. Loeb to Veblen, 16 August 1915.

Later in the war, Veblen wrote another book entitled *The Nature of Peace*. Again, he sent Loeb a copy of it and on 25 April 1917 received this reply:

> It is perfectly splendid and I might almost say better than any book you have written before if this were possible. . . . What you have not emphasized and what has impressed itself most deeply on me—and perhaps easterners in general—is the suspicion gained from the newspapers that the movement of preparedness involved by the war has after all as its main aim permanent militarism and compulsory military service for the sole purpose of crushing the labor movement completely and continuing the munition profits. The war spirit is confined in this country mainly to Wall Street and the University constituency. It is very amusing to see the reactionary papers of the east, like the *New York Times* and the *Sun* glorify the Russian Revolution, while at the same time they condemn any attempt at improving the lot of the American workingman.[51]

The radical tones in which Loeb wrote regarding the American drift toward war may provide evidence of the radicalizing influence of Veblen on him for a generation before the events of April, 1917 which brought formal entry into the struggle.

LOEB AND VEBLEN ON BERGSONIAN VITALISM

Loeb and Veblen both clearly belonged to the political Left which, at times, is quite evident in their correspondence. However, their intellectual similarities went deeper perhaps even to levels that can best be described as epistemological if not psychological. To illustrate, on 3 January 1919 Loeb wrote to Veblen to inform him that:

> I take pleasure in sending you a copy of my recent book on "Forced Movements, Tropisms and Animal Conduct" which I hope will interest you. You will see that I have entered upon the quixotic enterprise of bringing out a series of Biological Monographs in order to educate the younger generation into the spirit of exact quantitative experimentation. The book has been attacked in a recent number of the *Nation*, probably by some Bergsonian vitalist—the article was not signed and the writer was obviously extremely stupid since he or she did not

---

51. Loeb to Veblen, 3 January 1919.

understand or had not read the book.[52]

In 1914 in *The Instinct of Workmanship* Veblen, too, had commented in a massive footnote on what he regarded as the deficiencies of Henri Bergson's philosophy and Bergsonian vitalism. In the text immediately above the footnote he wrote:

> Neither the manner of life imposed by the machine process, nor the manner of thought inculcated by habituation to its logic, will fall in with the free movement of the human spirit, born, as it is, to fit the conditions of savage life. So, there comes an irrepressible—in a sense, congenital— recrudescence of magic, occult science, telepathy, spiritualism, vitalism, pragmatism.[53]

Then in the footnote below, which continued for several pages, he dissected Bergsonian vitalism by arguing, in effect, that it was a sophisticated form of animism, an opinion he shared with Loeb. As Veblen put it:

> The immanent, or rather intrinsically dominant, creative bent inherent in matter and not objectively distinguishable from it is sufficiently suggestive of that praeter—mechanical efficiency that seems so easy of comprehension to many of the peoples on the lower levels of culture, and that affords the substantial ground of magical practices and finds untroubled expression in the more naive of their theoretical speculations. It would be a work of extreme difficulty, e. g., to set up a consistently tenable distinction between M. Bergson's *elan de la vie*, on the one hand, and the *manna* of the Melanesians . . . the *wokonda* of the Sioux . . . or even the *hamingia* of Scandinavian paganism, on the other hand.[54]

---

52. Ibid. Pauly comments that "Loeb considered his 'mechanistic' position scientific common sense. It meant commitment to materialism and determinism, the belief that life could ultimately be explained in terms of physical science, an interest in physico-chemical methods, and the realization that ethical principles were ultimately grounded in biology." Pauly, *Controlling Life*, p. 141. Loeb invidiously contrasted the empirically based knowledge gotten through physical chemistry with "metaphysics" and "vitalistic mysticism." See Pauly, *Controlling Life*, pp. 139-40. Bergson's *Creative Evolution* had recently been translated from French and was the center of much controversy. Loeb thought Bergson's "elan vital" to be ridiculous and Veblen's opinion of it was also negative.

53. Veblen, *The Instinct of Workmanship*, p. 334.

54. Ibid.

VEBLEN'S ACADEMIC WOES

The story of Veblen's dismissals or forced resignations from at least two academic posts has been told many times, but perhaps in most detail by his biographer Joseph Dorfman.[55] It has never been directly told in his own words or those of his administrative adversaries. Veblen's correspondence with Loeb and the administrative archives at Chicago and Stanford, respectively, contain valuable information on the reasons for his departure from his first two jobs. On 10 February 1905, near the end of his thirteen year stay at Chicago, he wrote to Loeb that:

> I wish to leave Chicago as soon as I can and find a place to work elsewhere, and you might do me the best possible service by speaking to Mr. Jordan in my behalf. There is no university in America that I would prefer to Stanford. Mr. Jordan has in the past expressed the kindest regard for me, but I believe that in the present state of the Stanford finances it would take much urging to bring him to make an offer of any kind. Still, he may see his way to do so, and if you will burden yourself with speaking to him that will be the best possible way in which the matter could be brought to his attention. He already knows something of my work, and I believe the two men who are there in economics Messrs. McLean and [Harry] Millis, would be friendly to me.[56]

Veblen then explained in more detail to Loeb why he wished to leave Chicago:

> As to my reason for leaving here. I have never stood well with the president, and have been kept on the staff rather as a concession to Professor [James Laurence] Laughlin [Chairman of Department of Economics] than by the president's own choice. Lately, since last spring, his aversion has grown more settled, if not stronger; so that I am now staying here on sufferance and have been given notice that I need look for no recognition or advancement, but may be departed whenever it can be done without inconvenience. The president's growing dislike in connection with the scandalous gossip which has apparently reached you, being the cause of it rather than the effect. You are right in surmising that the gossip comes from Chicago, the

---

55. See Joseph Dorfman, *Thorstein Veblen and His America* (New York: Augustus M. Kelley, 1966) on Veblen's relationship with his wife. On his "womanizing" while he was at Stanford, see R. L. Duffus, *The Innocents at Cedro*, pp. 8, 18, 92, 98.

56. Veblen to Loeb, 10 February 1905.

center of diffusion being apparently his office in Haskell.[57]

It appears that President William Rainey Harper's dislike of Veblen was based on several events which occurred almost simultaneously as Veblen pointed out to Loeb in his letter of 10 February 1905.

> At the risk of lining you with loose talk I will give you an outline of the last half-year's adventures. They are not of such a character as to command belief on the part of anyone not familiar with the methods of our executive. By way of premise, during last year the wife of one of the faculty attended one of my courses of lectures. This man was also *persona non grata* with the president, at the same time that he is a friend of mine. Also, I had left over from the manuscript of the book on Business Enterprise a somewhat long chapter which offered an analysis of the working of business enterprise in the administration of a university. This chapter I proposed to publish as a separate small volume, and in the search for a publisher the manuscript came into the hands of the president. The argument was, of course, of an entirely impersonal character, but the president was apparently not pleased with it and seems to have seen in it some reflexions on the regime here.[58]

Veblen is clearly referring to *The Higher Learning in America* published many years later that contains a scathing indictment of the conduct of American universities by businessmen. In it, Veblen took delight in lampooning administrators like Harper but without mentioning them by name. But Harper's animosity because of it was not the end of the story. Veblen continues:

> At the close of the school year I went to Europe for the summer, as did also the man and woman spoken of above, with their child. Immediately after I had left the country—as I have learned since my return—reports were put in circulation that I had run away with the lady, and presumably with the man and the child. Hurried council was then taken to dismiss me from the university on the ground of my having brought the institution into disrepute. No intimation was given me of the proposed action, which after all failed to come to anything because the newspapers failed to print the reports given them. The matter being libellous, the papers refused to print it without someone among their informants who made up the

---

57. Ibid.

58. Ibid.

story, being also aware that it was libellous, and having nothing
to fall back on, were unwilling to vouch for it. So it fell through,
leaving nothing but an added degree of ill feeling between the
president and me, and such damage to my reputation as these
endeavors were calculated to yield. Under these circumstances
I should be glad to leave this place.[59]

Apparently, Loeb and Veblen's supporters at Stanford were
successful in persuading President David Starr Jordan to hire
Veblen for on 24 July 1906, Veblen wrote Loeb and his wife that he
expected to "leave Chicago next week and to reach California by
the middle of August, when I shall have an opportunity to tell you
both how deeply I appreciate my obligations to you for your good
offices in influencing Mr. Jordan."[60]

But Veblen's days at Stanford were short-lived and, in any
case, not altogether happy ones for, in order to obtain an
academic post there, he had to promise President Jordan that he
would bring his wife along and live with her. Veblen's exaggerated
reputation as a "womanizer" had preceded him and it was only a
short time until he was in trouble with the powers that be in Palo
Alto. He and his wife separated after he arrived and she showed
no inclination to rejoin him. President Jordan apparently heard
that Veblen was no longer living with his wife and called the
matter forcefully to his attention as a violation of the condition of
his employment. Veblen offered an explanation to Jordan,[61] but by
the fall of 1909, it was apparent that Veblen was in serious trouble
with the administration at Stanford. The gravity of his situation
was apparent in a letter he wrote to Loeb to thank him for his
support.[62] Whatever efforts, if any, were made by Loeb on his
behalf proved to be of no avail, however, and Veblen was forced to
find another academic post, this time at the University of Missouri
in Columbia. That university administrators used Veblen's
dalliances with women as a reason for firing him is beyond doubt.
Evidence of this is provided in a message written by the president
of Stanford to the president of the University of Chicago. In a
letter marked "confidential" David Starr Jordan told Henry Pratt
Judson that Veblen's philandering was offensive to academic

---

59. Ibid.

60. Veblen to Loeb, 24 July 1906.

61. See Veblen to David Starr Jordan, 19 November 1909, Stanford University
Archives, Cecil Green Library, Stanford, California.

62. Veblen to Loeb, 29 October 1909.

administrators.[63] However, the truth about Veblen's several dismissals from academic posts is more complex, for his ideological and political leanings may have influenced administrators against him. Veblen, also, expressed the perception that his commentary on the state of American higher education was a root cause of President Harper's animosity. Interestingly, President Jordan's later correspondence with Veblen indicates that he still read and admired Veblen's work and bore him no personal ill will.[64]

LOEB'S INFLUENCE ON VEBLEN

Another communication between Veblen and Loeb was dated 20 February 1913. In it, Veblen commented that:

> Since I last saw you I have been doing nothing substantially worth while and have published nothing, though there is manuscript for a small volume of theoretical speculations waiting for final revision and a possible publisher.[65]

Veblen was referring to what became *The Instinct of Workmanship* published in 1914 which, in his view, was his best book. The first part of the book was replete with citations of Loeb's work and that of other physiologists and evolutionary psychologists. Veblen's most polished and definitive statement on human nature and behavior is found here and it is evident that he has largely abandoned the instinctualist and racialist views that plagued him in *The Theory of the Leisure Class*.

That Veblen had considerable familiarity with Loeb's work is apparent both in *The Instinct of Workmanship* and in their correspondence. For many years they exchanged books and articles and the influence of each is occasionally evident in the writings of the other. To illustrate this point, on 20 February 1913 Veblen wrote to Loeb:

> I thank you much for the copy of *The Mechanistic Conception of Life*, which has lately come to hand from the publishers. I had already made acquaintance with the volume and need not tell

---

63. See David S. Jordan to Henry P. Judson, 6 October 1909, University Presidents Papers, 1889-1925, Regenstein Library, University of Chicago, Chicago, Illinois.

64. See David S. Jordan to Thorstein Veblen, 22 August 1917, Thorstein Veblen Collection, Wisconsin State Historical Society, Madison, Wisconsin.

65. Veblen to Loeb, 24 March 1905.

you how greatly I value these papers of yours, several (or at least two) of which I had not seen before they appeared in the books.[66]

The last book of Veblen's on which Loeb commented in their correspondence was *The Higher Learning in America*. On 3 January 1919, Loeb wrote:

> Thanks very much for your kindness in sending me your new book on "Higher Learning" two chapters of which I read immediately with the greatest enjoyment. I think it is a most welcome and necessary book which I hope will bring good results. Science and research can be thoroughly grateful to you for the vigorous plea you have made on their behalf. I am also delighted with your stand in regard to vocational training.[67]

Loeb refers in the last sentence to Veblen's strongly stated belief expressed in *The Higher Learning in America* that, although certain kinds of vocational education might have some social value, they have no place in the curriculum of a real university. This was but a restatement of his long-held belief that a university exists to further the life of the mind and this is done most effectively through the social studies, humanities and natural sciences. Loeb apparently shared Veblen's conviction that the learning process is badly eroded by vocationalization and the university atmosphere itself contaminated by courses aimed at inducing commercial predation in the students.

CONCLUSION

The movement toward reductionism in the natural sciences played an important role in biology and it is exemplified in Loeb's description of a tropism. However, Veblen clearly did not believe that tropisms were adequate explanations of the wider ranges of human behavior. They could not, for example, explain parenting, pride and skill in work, or critical inquiry much less art, music or poetry. Tropismatic behavior itself only took on social or cultural significance in broader institutional complexes when "habits" were formed and so human behavior was not explicable in solely or even largely tropismatic terms. For Veblen, particularly in his later works, behavior is not reducible to physico-chemical processes occurring

66. Veblen to Loeb, 20 February 1913.

67. Loeb to Veblen, 3 January 1919.

in the brain and the nervous system as is so patently the case in much of Loeb's work. Rather, in Veblen's writings, and certainly in that of his Chicago colleague John Dewey, culturally salient human behavior is explicable only in biological *and* social terms. However sympathetic Veblen may have been toward Loeb's scientific research, inductivism and political attitudes, he did not endorse his more extreme mechanistic physiological claims.

Loeb shared Veblen's sympathy for socialism as well as his dislike of nationalism, militarism and racism. He may also have possessed some of Veblen's positive attitudes toward the emancipation of women, although he was less explicit about this. Loeb was offended by the movement of biology toward mysticism, metaphysics and, as he believed, "collusion with socially and politically destructive elements."[68] He came to see biological romanticism "at the root of nationalism, militarism, and anti-Semitism."[69] The war had severely damaged Loeb's social and political hopes and he came to believe that the war was the start of "a new dark age."[70] This then led to a permanent withdrawal from electoral politics, for "in the years after the war Loeb became a stereotype of the ivory-tower scientist."[71] But the war and its immediate aftermath had a different effect on Veblen for he became for a time more of an activist. His published work was more polemical than it had ever been before and was aimed at wider audiences perhaps in hopes of influencing the course of events.

Although the extant correspondence between Loeb and Veblen ends in 1919, they may have continued to communicate with each other until Loeb's death in 1924. In any case it is evident that a considerable mutual influence existed with Loeb impacting on Veblen's views of human nature and behavior and Veblen, in turn, possibly exerting a radicalizing influence on Loeb's politics and economics. Loeb's possible influence on Veblen's appointment by President Jordan at Stanford and his apparent defense of him when he got into trouble left Veblen permanently in his debt.

The moral attitudes prevalent among faculty and administrators at western universities today make it difficult to understand or sympathize with Veblen's treatment by Presidents Harper and Jordan. In any case, Veblen's political views and ideological

---

68. Ibid., 25 April 1917.

69. Pauly, *Controlling Life*, p. 154.

70. Ibid., p. 160.

71. Ibid., pp. 160-61.

perspective did not generally ingratiate him with administrators and his "womanizing" provided ample opportunity for getting rid of him on grounds that, at the time, did not seem to infringe directly on academic freedom.[72] The Loeb-Veblen correspondence thus provides insight not only into the development of their own thought, but illuminates the social mores and ethical standards imposed on at least two leading academic institutions by their presidents. It also gives evidence of the fragility of academic freedom and freedom of inquiry and the fine line that separated these from the right of academics to enjoy their own life-style.

It is interesting to note that Loeb even made his way into American literature in a major way in the 1925 novel *Arrowsmith* by Sinclair Lewis. Lewis, the first American winner of the Nobel Prize in literature in 1930, and author of such acclaimed novels as *Main Street* (1920) and *Babbitt* (1922), became acquainted with Dr. Paul de Kruif, who for a time had been Loeb's colleague at the Rockefeller Institute in New York City after World War I. Lewis and de Kruif met in 1922, the same year De Kruif ended his relationship with the Institute to pursue a literary career. The two became fast friends and traveled to the West Indies and Europe together while de Kruif provided vast amounts of information to Lewis about the medical profession and scientific research. This input came to fruition in Lewis's *Arrowsmith* in which Loeb plays a major role as Dr. Max Gottlieb, an eccentric scientist of German-Jewish background. Gottlieb, as portrayed by Lewis, is too alienated from American life and culture and too impractical and impolitic to be an exact replica of Loeb. Nevertheless, the affinity is clear for he is of an ideal-typical scientific genius, oblivious at times to the external world while grossly absorbed in his laboratory experiments. The lengthy novel focuses on a twenty-year span in the life of Martin Arrowsmith from the time he was a young medical student to his leaving the medical profession to become an experimental biologist in an isolated laboratory in the woods. It is clear that Lewis has two favorites in the book and they are Gottlieb and Arrowsmith who ultimately models

---

72. The Chicago philosopher George H. Mead once wrote to his wife that he "had a pleasant call upon Veblen, who is pained because the Socialist Review says his doctrine is good socialism." It is unlikely that Veblen would have made such a comment on grounds of ideological conviction given his sympathies for socialism; rather, it is probably evidence of the tenuous nature of academic freedom and tenure at the University of Chicago in its early years. G. H. Mead to Helen Mead, 13 May 1901, Mead Collection, Regenstein Library, University of Chicago. It is also worth mentioning that Veblen's colleague Edward Bemis had been unable to secure reappointment as associate professor of political economy ostensibly because his attitudes on public utility regulation were offensive to the local utility magnate. See Joseph Dorfman, *Thorstein Veblen and His America*, pp. 122-23.

himself after his old professor by becoming completely absorbed in the pursuit of scientific idle curiosity and remaining oblivious to the things of this world.[73]

Finally, it appears that Veblen, by all accounts, was also a great influence on Sinclair Lewis so that the latter's novels reflect the impact of both Veblen's and Loeb's thought. Loeb's ideas are thus embedded in the novels of America's first Nobel Prize winner in literature and in the thought of its most influential heterodox economist. But we shall leave it to others to uncover and delineate Loeb's influence on still other social scientists and humanists of his time.

---

73. See Barbara Grace Spayd's biographical sketch of Sinclair Lewis in his *Arrowsmith* (New York: Harcourt, Brace and Company, 1952) pp. V-XXI.

Jacques Loeb: His Science and Social Activism

CHAPTER SIX
LOEB ON RACISM, ZIONISM AND ETHNOCENTRISM

———•———

INTRODUCTION

Loeb defended Asiatics against the exclusion laws and discriminatory practices that threatened them and he took the side of blacks against the Jim Crow laws passed in many states between 1890 and 1910. Especially during the Great War, he attacked the Imperial German regime and its apologists for their unwarranted claims of racial and cultural superiority. To illustrate this last point, the linkage between Loeb's own scientific work and his political views was much in evidence in a letter he wrote on 11 March 1918 to the eminent English physicist Ernest Rutherford: He commented to Rutherford that German biology was "antiquated" and was a "pseudo-biology" used to justify mistreatment of other ethnic groups, "like the Armenians, the Jews, the English." Loeb stated that the German scientists used their biology to differentiate "racial" groups, and then assign hierarchical status according to some notion of inferior vs. superior "races" with Germans occupying the latter category, of course. Loeb also criticized German biology for what he saw as its tendency of "reverting continually to the antiquated philosophy of Kant."[1]

To summarize the thrust of Loeb's comments; first, the German scientific community, or at least a significant part of it, was at fault for promulgating doctrines of racial elitism that had no basis in scientific biology; second, German idealist philosophy was not empirical in the sense of using quantitative-statistical or experimental methods which were congruent with science, and third, the German ruling caste and militarists used all of the above to rationalize their brutal aggression.

In an undated three–page handwritten manuscript which was either a memoranda to himself or a condensation of a public lecture entitled "Heredity and Racial Inferiority", Loeb argued as follows: mental and moral traits are not linked with race through genetic transmission. Intelligence and moral control, for example, are thus not racial in nature. Racial intermarriage does not lead to

---

1. Loeb to Ernest Rutherford, 11 March 1918.

degeneracy; rather the experiments of Luther Burbank and others with heterozygosity indicate that race mixture may actually improve the breed. (The term applied to this phenomenon today is "hybrid vigor." Loeb was indeed aware of developments across the range of sciences—Burbank's genetic experiments involved plants.) Loeb thus concluded that: "It is not only contrary to justice but also contrary to scientific facts to deny the colored people, equal rights and equal economic, social and educational facilities with the whites."[2]

On 22 March 1915, Loeb spoke at a symposium of the Socialist Press Club in New York City. He asked his audience whether racial antagonism was an inherited instinct, or an artificial product brought about by human conditions, and in response to his own question concluded it was the latter. On this occasion, however, his targets were racists who advocated discrimination against or exclusion of Asiatics from American soil. The charges against the Japanese were the usual ones made against racial minorities. They were clannish, sexually immoral, and unethical in business. Furthermore, they were willing to work for low wages which thus lowered the standard of living for the white working class. Indeed, it was Loeb's hypothesis that racial antagonism had no biological basis, but arose purely on the basis of economic conflict. Since Loeb was addressing a group of socialists he asked rhetorically:

> Now then what can Socialism do in this situation? I think if the Socialist Party is the party which stands for justice—and I think that is the right definition; at least that is the definition of it which appeals to me—it is natural that the Socialist Party should say, "We cannot refuse sympathy to a human being when he suffers outside of a certain geographical boundary, anymore than when he is inside." I think the Socialist Party, if it is true to its principles is bound to say "We cannot tolerate racial antagonism."[3]

The title of Loeb's address which was "Can Socialism Obliterate Race Antagonism?" thus was answered at least tentatively in the affirmative.

Another short piece Loeb wrote which might have been used as an address to some group of civic-minded citizens was entitled "Pseudoscience and Ruthlessness." It was an indictment of the German racial biology which rested on two main laws. The first law

2. Loeb, "Heredity and Racial Inferiority," p. 3.

3. Loeb, "Can Socialism Obliterate Race Antagonism?", pp. 8-9.

was that "the Germans are the noblest of all races." The second was that "by mixture with any other 'race' the Germans are bound to deteriorate, on the basis of an alleged law of heredity according to which the hybrid inherits only the bad qualities of the parents, while the good ones disappear."[4] Loeb argued that the humanitarian attitudes of the German people had been largely eradicated by a "literary campaign of brutalization started by Bismarck and his tool [Heinrich] von Treitschke for purely political purposes," and this campaign focused on creating animosity and disrespect for other nations and "races." Loeb charged that the biologists such as Duhring who provided the Imperial government with its German racial biology were scientifically incompetent and ignorant of modern biology. Despite their ignorance and charlatanism they played a key role in providing a rationale for German imperialism and militarism. There was no denying their responsibility for bringing about an attitude of apathy and indifference on the part of the German masses toward such atrocities as the Armenian massacres by the Turks.

This last claim was Loeb's response to Germany's ignoring the massive atrocities inflicted by the Turks in 1915 on their Armenian minority. Turkey had been Germany's ally during the Great War. Loeb's dislike of racism was based on more than moral and scientific grounds, although these were very important to him. Rather, much of his animus was directed against it on political grounds because it was both a cause and a rationale for militarism, imperialism and war. This was most evident in a letter he wrote to his friend Arrhenius in Stockholm in 1914. The latter was a Swedish citizen and since Sweden was neutral, Loeb found him a sympathetic listener. In this letter Loeb took to task the Germans and the Russians ("and possibly . . . other countries") for propagandizing within their respective borders the notion of ethnic superiority or as Loeb termed it "racial superiority," the notion of race being used to specify a particular national group such as "the Germans." Loeb argued that such "racial" antagonisms were the cause of conflicts between nations and even within nations and that if allowed to continue after the war would surely reignite future wars; he proposed to Arrhenius "that as soon as this war is over we shall have to begin a campaign against the racial conceit which has been fostered systematically in Germany, Russia . . . [and] tolerated if not supported by their governments." Loeb was not content simply to discover such evils abroad. In a scathing indictment of his own adopted country, Loeb pointed to

---

4. Loeb, "Pseudoscience and Ruthlessness," p. 2.

the problems in this country involving African-Americans and Japanese-Americans; "Here too we are having no end of difficulties caused by the fanatical maltreatment of the Negro and the Japanese."[5]

Loeb's commitment to racial equality was fully evident in his correspondence with other scientists particularly when he felt that one of his scientific colleagues was guilty of racism. In 1916 one such incident occurred and Loeb wrote to Frank Lillie, a scientist at the University of Chicago that:

> I do not know whether you have read the paper by [J. E.] Wodsedalek in the last number of the BIOLOGICAL BULLETIN, which on page 13, in the last paragraph, contains the following two sentences which I believe have nothing to do with the contents of his paper or with science in general, and which are an insult to the Negro. The one statement is "but unfortunately the mulatto is fertile," and a second statement a little above this is "the Negro is fully as far removed from the white man as is the ass from the horse." It seems to me that on account of the unfortunate conditions of prejudice under which the Negro's life is made miserable, the editors of the BIOLOGICAL BULLETIN should not allow these passages to go by without a disavowal and a statement that Wodsedalek has abused his privilege of hospitality in the BIOLOGICAL BULLETIN, by utilizing the standing of the BIOLOGICAL BULLETIN to give vent to his personal animosity against the Negro, I do not know who this man Wodsedalek is—I have never heard of him before, whether he is a southerner—but I think things of that kind should not be tolerated to creep into scientific journals.[6]

For a couple of months Loeb continued to correspond with Thomas Hunt Morgan and Lillie about the incident. He was fearful not only that black scientists might be offended by it, but that antiblack fanatics might seize upon it to justify their bigotry and antiblack activism. However, on 6 March 1916, the incident came to a close when he responded to a letter from Lillie:

> Thanks for your letter from Wodsedalek which I herewith return. I am glad to know that he did not intend to insult the Negro. However, he is quite mistaken if he thinks that it was impossible to misunderstand his meaning. I was afraid that his sentences might be utilized as material for further persecution of the Negro. His disavowal of such an

5. Loeb to Svante Arrhenius, 14 December 1914.

6. Loeb to Frank Lillie, 2 February 1916.

interpretation of his remarks I think will act as a sufficient safeguard against such a possibility.[7]

Judging from his correspondence with W. E. B. Dubois, director of publicity and research, and Oswald Garrison Villard, treasurer of the National Association for the Advancement of Colored People, respectively, Loeb was in demand as a speaker for civil rights groups.[8]

HYBRIDS AND RACIAL INTERMARRIAGE

Loeb was very outspoken against racism in any form and attempted to use biological arguments to combat it. Other opponents of racism were aware of this and asked him on various occasions to participate in organized opposition to racist policies. One such individual was Harvey H. Guy, professor of the History of Christianity and Religion at the Pacific Theological Seminary in Berkeley, California who wrote to Loeb in 1914 to solicit his aid. In this communication Guy described an organization in San Francisco known as the Japan Society of America. The express purpose of the organization was to foster better relations between Americans and Japanese; the organization sponsored regular speakers on relevant topics and was in the process of initiating the publication of a monthly bulletin. His request to Loeb was that the latter prepare a piece for the bulletin addressing, from a biological point of view, the topics of Japanese immigration to the West Coast and of intermarriage between Japanese-American immigrants and non-Japanese Americans. Anticipating that the intermarriage topic might prove too controversial, Guy offered Loeb the option of deleting it from his offering.[9] Loeb was his usual outspoken self in replying to Guy:

> I do not hesitate to state that there is no biological objection to any race mixture. The general statement that the mixture of races leads to degeneracy is not corroborated by fact. On the contrary, the investigations of Burbank, Shull and East have shown that, in certain cases at least, the hybrid is stronger and

7. Ibid., 6 March 1916.

8. See Oswald Garrison Villard to Loeb, 29 April 1914 and Loeb to W. E. B. Dubois, 13 October 1914.

9. Harvey Guy to Loeb, 11 March 1914.

more resistant than either of the parent forms. I am, therefore, of the opinion that the question of intermarriage is entirely a private affair of the two individuals concerned.[10]

Charles Eliot, president of Harvard from 1869 to 1909, who probably shared Loeb's views on the subject, exchanged letters with him. It is interesting to note, however, that some of Loeb's arguments were cultural and moral in addition to being genetic. In a letter to Elliot written early in 1915, Loeb discussed the issue of interracial relations between sexes, both with and without the formality of marriage. Loeb allowed that the offspring of such interracial relations often involve "a large percentage of degenerates" by which he apparently meant individuals who were less than successful in finding work or a comfortable and stable niche in society. However, he argued that the adjustment problems of the offspring of interracial pairings are "not on account of the racial mixture." He pointed to two main causes of problems for these children. First, he suggests that individuals who elect to enter such interracial relationships are probably already marginalized within their own racial communities and therefore among the least fit to become parents in the first place; he concludes "that if the same element were chosen for breeding purposes from one and the same race the result would probably be just as bad." The second factor that Loeb points to in causing problems for the offspring of interracial pairings is the presumed low quality of the environment in which the children are raised; as he put it, they "not only suffer from bad heredity but they also suffer from poor surroundings." Loeb blamed several factors for such "poor surroundings," including unfit mothers, that is, mothers whose care of the children is deficient for reasons totally unrelated to race or racial mixture, absent fathers, and in particular, in Loeb's view, the "stigma of illegitimacy." It was his observation that interracial pairings were in most cases illegitimate and that this factor alone, independent of racial factors, was a major source of problems related to the well-being of the children."[11]

In an immediate letter of response, Elliot added some penetrating comments of his own concerning the problem. He built on the themes in Loeb's letter of the previous day when he (Elliot) added that a very important problem for these children "another handicap besides those you mention—they grow up in an atmosphere of contempt—a very depressing thing for any human

10. Loeb to Harvey Guy, 20 May 1914.

11. Loeb to Charles Eliot, 9 February 1915.

being. This contempt is visited on the legitimate as well as on the illegitimate. "Elliot continues in this letter by describing the strengths and weaknesses of various racial pairings in a manner many would find startling today, because his conclusions focus solely on racial characteristics to the virtual exclusion of the personal characteristics of the individuals involved. His comments include "while fathers of Eurasians are generally poor specimens . . .," that "the best mixed breed . . . was the cross of the Chinese man with the Hawaiian woman," and that their offspring, ". . . make good citizens . . . diligent and trustworthy workmen," and further that, ". . . the Chinese father . . . brings up his children better than the white man does."[12]

A year earlier Loeb had summarized his views on the subject in the following way. First, modern work in genetics had shown that hereditary traits were as a rule not linked together, but were transmitted independent of each other. Skin and eye color were, therefore, not necessarily connected with lesser intelligence or moral character. Loeb conceded, however, that much remained to be learned regarding the heredity of mental and moral traits. Nevertheless, he did not believe that racial intermarriage or mixture of races lead necessarily to degeneracy. Indeed, he argued that with some exceptions hybridization often improved a breed. He, therefore, felt that it was contrary to scientific facts and to justice to deny blacks equal rights and access to economic, social and educational facilities with the white race.[13] He clearly had in mind the practices implemented by Jim Crow laws in the southern states between 1890 and 1910 and subsequently reinforced by further legislation and informal discriminatory practices. Although Loeb did not live to see it, one is reminded of the ordinance adopted in Birmingham, Alabama, in 1930 which made it illegal for blacks and whites to play checkers and dominoes together.[14]

Loeb was not just interested in combating racism and racial inequality as important as these were in his political and scientific agenda. His goals were even broader than these. In a 1921 letter to a friend, Loeb once again raised the alarm against "Eugenics—or rather a caricature of eugenics, so called 'Racial Biology'," which he felt was being used as a basis for directing fear and hatred on the part of one racial, ethnic or national group against another. In

---

12. Charles Eliot to Loeb, 10 February 1915.

13. See Loeb's article in "*The Crisis,*" Vol. 8, No. 2 (June, 1914): 85.

14. See C. Van Woodward, *The Strange Career of Jim Crow* (New York: Oxford University Press, 1966).

pointing to the writings of H. G. Wells, Loeb paraphrased the latter in saying, "if we wish to [save] humanity we have to work towards cooperation, unification, and first of all tolerance." It should be noted, he had no doubt which individuals were spreading racial hatred and pseudo-scientific rationalizations. Loeb identified individual culprits in Germany, "the Houston Chamberlains," in America, "Madison Grant" as well as organizations like the "Ku-Klux-Klan." Loeb inquires of his correspondent, "I wonder whether you have read Well's *Outline of History*. I think it a wonderful book and what he says about unification of humanity seems . . . the gospel by which further catastrophes can be averted." Again, Loeb not only condemns the social effects of "racial biology," but also castigates its claims as contrary to the current findings of the sciences of physical chemistry and biology.[15]

Loeb did not merely locate the doctrinal sources of racial hatred in the writings of certain right-wing intellectuals. He also identified powerful and eminent educators as major sources of discord. He was particularly critical of Germany and Russia. In the former he pointed to anthropologists, German literature, "the reptile press" and once again, the racist propagandist Houston Stewart Chamberlain. Moreover, "The massacre of the Armenians was conducted with the active cooperation of the German officers." He condemns the Russians for their mass murders of the Jews during the Romanoff Dynasty, another atrocity he saw as being encouraged by the Germans, buttressed by their concepts of racial superiority in the form of racial Darwinism. Loeb reviewed these observations in a 1918 letter to Dr. Maurice Caullery of France; he also focused attentively on visiting American educators, particularly President Nicholas Murray Butler of Columbia and President Benjamin Ide Wheeler of the University of California. Loeb charged, at least in his letter to Caullery, that these academics were significantly influenced by the racial ideas of the Germans, to such an extent that they "became the agents of the Emperor and the Junkers in spreading this race propaganda in America; of course in a quiet way." The intensity of Loeb's feelings on the matter are revealed in his comment, "so eager was President Butler in his propaganda for the German Emperor that he got into an actual quarrel with the late Prof. Munsterberg as to who should have parasitic precedence with the Emperor." Loeb expressed concern that a similar form of "Prussian anti-Semitism" was being furthered in some circles of higher education in this country, not as blatantly as in Germany or Russia, "but they are being done just

15. Loeb to S. J. Holmes, 11 October 1921.

the same."[16] It goes without saying, of course, that perhaps more than any other social or political issues, except those of war and peace, nothing was as vital to Loeb as discrediting racism. That Loeb aimed his scientific work at an audience broader than just the scientific community is apparent in his correspondence.[17]

THE ERNEST JUST EPISODE

Loeb's attitudes toward racism and racist doctrine have been described in some detail already. He was keenly aware of the injustices done to blacks by whites in almost every walk of American life. Loeb was an ardent advocate, however, not just of achieving better understanding between races, but of improving the quality of life for black people especially in the American South. Given his humanitarian outlook and his doctorate from Strassburg in medicine, it is not surprising that he focused on the improvement of health care. In a revealing manner, Loeb dealt with some of these medical issues in a 1914 letter to a Jerome D. Greene, a potential financial contributor to Howard Medical School. Loeb stated that one of the most severe deficiencies in the social environment of the black underclass was in the area of health care particularly in the South where "I do not believe . . . white physicians care to practice among negroes, and if so, I do not think that negroes care in many cases to be treated by their white oppressors." He extolled Howard Medical School as being the only medical school in the country dedicated to providing quality training to future African-American physicians. He felt the need was great and that "well trained physicians are the best missionaries for uplift that could be sent to the negro." It may be a sign of the times that Loeb, in this letter,

---

16. Loeb to Dr. Maurice Caullery, 4 February 1918.

17. Both his motives and the breadth of his audience was revealed in a letter he wrote to a former colleague at the University of California, Berkeley.

> Please accept my sincere thanks for your kind review of my book on "Forced Movements, Tropisms, and Animal Conduct" in the *New Republic*. Several years ago [Editor Herbert] Croly asked me to recommend somebody who could give them from time to time notes on scientific topics in a style sufficiently literary to satisfy the fastidious taste of the staff and readers of the *New Republic*. I recommended you and Torrey. From your review I am glad to see that Croly acted upon my recommendation. I hope that in the interest of the scientific education of our reading public you will continue to write for the *New Republic*. It seems to me very important for a democratic country that the progress of exact science should be brought to their attention.

Loeb to S. J. Holmes, 11 October 1921.

does not mention the possibility of making direct use of other established (white) medical schools to help meet the need; but, if the intent of the letter was to solicit funds for Howard, it may simply not have been seen as a helpful comment. In any case, Loeb goes on to point out that financial support for this one medical training facility would do more "for the uplift of the negro" than an equal contribution used in any other way.[18]

Since Ernest Just's relationship with Loeb has been dealt with elsewhere in some detail only a few comments are in order. Just's biographer, the historian of science, Kenneth R. Manning, has alleged that Just was the victim of racial discrimination and that Loeb was a key figure in frustrating his career goals.[19] Seymour S. Cohen has summarized Manning's case in these words:

> Despite his experimental contributions in summers at Woods Hole, Just was unable to join the faculty of a university that encouraged the research activities of its teaching staff. He was constrained to spend most of each academic year teaching undergraduates at Howard University, a major institution of higher learning for blacks in Washington, D.C. Although Just obtained grants to support his work, assistants and even travel, he sought and was turned down for positions at various prestigious research-oriented institutions. His attempt to move included an application to Simon Flexner at the Rockefeller Institute for Medical Research in 1923. This evoked a vigorous and uncomplimentary dissent from Jacques Loeb, whose work in artificial parthenogenesis and newer studies on protein reactivities had been criticized by Just and several of Just's associates. It should be noted that in 1914 and 1915, a vociferously antiracist Loeb had assisted Just. Nevertheless by 1923 Loeb had denounced a presumably "arrogant" and "incompetent" Just, an act imputed to be racist by Manning. Although Loeb died in 1924, Just's frustrations with American universities and institutes continued for many years.[20]

Loeb's papers contain a considerable correspondence with and about Ernest Just. As early as 1914, he described Just and his

---

18. Loeb to Jerome D. Greene, 17 October 1914.

19. See Kenneth R. Manning, *Black Apollo of Science: The Life of Ernest Everett Just* (New York: Oxford University Press, 1983). Also, see the account by Pauly in *Controlling Life*, pp. 154, 156-60.

20. Seymour S. Cohen, "Balancing Science and History: A Problem of Scientific Biography," *History and Philosophy of the Life Sciences*, 8 (1986): 122. It should be noted that Cohen does not think Manning makes a persuasive case against Loeb on racial grounds.

situation in a plea to the Rockefeller Foundation for funding in support of the Howard Medical School. Once again he praised Howard as the nation's only medical school "of sufficiently high standing" dedicated to the training of "colored" physicians. To buttress his argument for funding for Howard, Loeb provided a highly favorable description of Just who was teaching physiology there and whom Loeb described as "certainly a superior man." He admiringly pointed to Just's education at "Dartmouth, where he took his degree with high honors," to his modest salary, only a small portion of which he was actually receiving (presumably due to Howard's impecunious financial condition), to Just's idealism, to his intelligence and to his cultivation. Then Loeb states, "I plead very earnestly for this cause, because I am really convinced that it would be difficult to find anything that could be more deserving of support, and . . . I know . . . the Rockefeller Foundation is above that racial prejudice which would deny help to colored people."[21] This concluding sentence is difficult to reconcile with any description of Loeb as harboring racial animosity toward Ernest Just.

At first, Just appears to have been genuinely grateful to Loeb for the opportunity to work with him at the Marine Biological Laboratory at Woods Hole, Massachusetts. In the fall of 1914, in fact, Just wrote Loeb to thank him for his support and his words ring true with pathos. Just exclaims, "I shall never forget 1914 at Woods Hole." He goes on to thank Loeb profusely for his kindnesses and describes him as a source of great personal inspiration. In the letter, Just reveals what seems to be a pained awareness of his own racial disadvantage when he says, "We colored men are very much like dumb animals; we appreciate kindness and interest," and again with the comment "after a chat with you one night as I was leaving my work, I felt almost human and a part of the world that is living."[22]

In his reply to this letter a few days later, Loeb made laudatory comments to Just which clearly indicate an extremely positive view of the younger man. Loeb expressed great pleasure and satisfaction over their relationship at Woods Hole the previous summer and expressed hope that they could make contact at the same place during the next summer. He remarked that he (Loeb) had learned a great deal from their interpersonal interactions. Loeb went on to say that he had discussed Just's college with both Simon and Abraham Flexner, presumably with the goal of encouraging financial support. He expressed great confidence in Just's personal future development and concluded with the following uplifting

---

21. Loeb to Jerome D. Greene, 17 October 1914.

22. Ernest Just to Loeb, 12 October 1914.

sentiment, "I do not know anything more beautiful than to devote oneself to an unselfish cause . . . which in the long run is bound to win, though you and I may not live to see that day."[23]

The common ground shared by Loeb and Just is obvious: both favored a multiracial society in which blacks, whites and other races could coexist on a footing of equality; to achieve this end, they believed, would require a removal of discriminatory laws and informal racist practices. But this convergence of goals and ideals does not answer the question as to whether or not Loeb mistreated Just because of his race as Kenneth Manning has charged.

Nevertheless, it might be useful to juxtapose quotations from Loeb's private correspondence in order to better understand the change over time in Loeb's attitudes toward Just. The first quotation is from a letter written to the secretary of the National Association for the Advancement of Colored People in 1914:

> While I heartily sympathize with the objects of the National Association for the Advancement of Colored People, and while I am ready to contribute towards its support in any way I can, I know only so few of the colored people that I feel a recommendation might do injustice to those I do not know. But with this proviso I would suggest that the medal be given to one of the few colored people who, in the face of great difficulties, are doing research work in science. One of the men I have in mind is Mr. Just, Professor of Physiology at Howard University, whom I know personally very well and of whom I know that he is a very able research worker. Mr. Just has sacrificed a good deal for the advancement of the medical schools for colored people, and he will do a good deal more if he is given a chance as I hope he may be.[24]

Although the next letter to be quoted from was written to a different individual for somewhat different reasons, its very tone resonates in another direction. Marked "confidential," it suggests that Loeb's attitudes toward Just have changed significantly in the intervening six–year period.

> Since I gather from your letter that I may have been indirectly responsible for Dr. Just's National Research Fellowship, I feel that it is only just to you that I express myself with complete frankness. I do not think that Just will ever be a prominent investigator, but I think he can be made a better type of

23. Loeb to Ernest Just, 16 October 1914.

24. Loeb to May Childs Nerney, 24 September 1914.

scientific teacher through his research fellowship. Instead of going to Jamaica, continuing the type of work he is doing at present, and which I consider not of a high type, I think it would be better for him to stay in Washington and use the freedom granted him by his fellowship for developing along the lines of physical chemistry and organic chemistry. If, with that knowledge, he continues his present line of research his work will be at least of a better character. Since Just is hypersensitive, it might be well not to mention the fact to him that you consulted me in this matter.[25]

Nevertheless, on the basis of the information available to Loeb scholars, it does not appear that he acted as he did toward Just on the basis of racial bias. Indeed, what is evident in most of Loeb's disputes with other scientists is that he was extremely tenacious in defending and advancing his own scientific work. While Just may have thought Loeb was racially motivated, it was easy for him to overlook both the pride Loeb took in his own work and his extraordinary competence as a laboratory experimentalist. On the whole, we agree with the more balanced and judicious Cohen treatment of the Loeb-Just relationship rather than with Manning. On the one hand, Loeb's work had evoked the delighted approbation of the investigators oriented to biophysical chemistry. However, among, the colloidologists, Loeb was described as having a "sterilizing influence" and men such as Mathews were being urged to spend their summers at the newer laboratory at Cold Spring Harbor. In a bitter and sarcastic letter to W. J. V. Osterhout in 1921, Loeb expressed the hope that Mathews, Just and some others would indeed go to "the exhilarating atmosphere of Cold Spring Harbor" and not "be stifled by (his) proximity." In this letter also he refers to some recent work which shows that "there was much less merit to the speculations of colloid chemistry than I even admitted."[26]

In brief, then, the split between Loeb and Just developed, in Loeb's view at least, largely around scientific issues. To paraphrase Cohen, Just, following in the path of his teachers, Frank Lillie and Albert P. Mathews, and a youthful colleague, L. V. Heilbrunn, had decided not to pursue the chemical studies which were beginning to restructure biochemistry and biological thought. Loeb's assistants John Howard Northrop and Moses Kunitz were soon to transform enzymology by the isolation, crystallization and molecular characterization of key enzymes. Indeed, some of these discoveries, as well as the body of their work, became fundamental

---

25. Loeb to Abraham Flexner, 11 November 1920.

26. Loeb to W. J. V. Osterhout, 21 February 1921.

to the evolution of molecular biology, which is now revolutionizing embryology.

> Manning's book does not provide an insight into these large scientific issues. Just's turmoil is portrayed as personal and doomed in a setting of racial segregation. The portrayal has neglected the key roles of influential participants, such as Mathews, and of scientific orientation, such as the major differences of Loeb on the one hand and of Mathews and Just on the other. Furthermore, it is impossible to conjecture to what extent the interaction of personal antagonism and scientific differences of these individuals may have influenced the various events. Manning's sympathetic portrayal of the tragic Just as a lone black biologist seeking recognition and fame in a white community and defeated by racism is important but incomplete in several crucial respects described above; the book is therefore seriously flawed. The case of Just emphasizes the need to portray the man fully in the science of his time and the scientist as embattled in the human condition.[27]

Loeb was a strongly assertive personality, particularly when it came to disagreements about fundamental scientific issues. He was occasionally short and brusque with those individuals who disagreed with him. At times, he viewed the opposing party in such disagreements, at least disagreements on fundamental issues, as lacking in intelligence or competence. Ernest Just would not be the only scientist to encounter this side of Jacques Loeb. We find this a far more convincing explanation of the conflict between the two than racial prejudice.

ANTI-SEMITISM AND ZIONISM

Loeb, himself, was of Jewish origin but completely secularized and, in any case, married to a woman of the old New England Protestant stock. Although without any apparent affinity for Judaism in any of its forms, he was, nevertheless, sensitive to the crude and degrading effects of anti-Semitism. He commented in a letter to Wolfgang Pauli that he considered anti-Semitism to be an ominous signal for the future of any nation because it was "a symptom of degradation" and, "a symptom of brutality." Loeb was dismayed by the behavior of the

27. See Cohen "Balancing Science and History: A Problem of Scientific Biography," pp. 121-28, esp. p. 128. Also, see Cohen, "Some Struggles of Jacques Loeb, Albert Mathews and Ernest Just at the Marine Biological Laboratory," *Biological Bulletin,* 168 (Supplement) (June 1985): 127-36.

Hungarian government and he predicted that Hungary because of brutal anti-Semitism "will not gain the sympathy of the foreign countries, even in countries which are ruled by a brutal capitalism."[28]

For many years Loeb was employed by the Rockefeller Institute for Medical Research in New York City. During his stay there he was blackballed by the Century Club when he applied for membership apparently because he was Jewish. He wrote to his friend, Columbia psychologist James McKeen Cattell, who had sponsored his membership, that it had been a mistake for him (Loeb) to have considered membership in the first place in an elitist "snobocracy." Loeb also was willing to tell his friend that "you made a mistake belonging to such a club." He concluded from the whole affair that "the traditions of a social and intellectual aristocracy may move forward to democratic usefulness, but they are more likely to degenerate."[29] It seems that this sequence of events involving the Century Club reinforced Loeb's perceptions of a growing anti-Semitism in American culture even among the educated and the elite.

Like many intellectuals of Jewish origin, Loeb was not only sensitive about anti-Semitism but also curious about Zionism, although he was skeptical of the motives and programs of the Zionist leaders. In 1923, he wrote to Arrhenius to complain of the racial environment in the United States and made some revealing comments about corporate leaders known to be anti-Semitic. Loeb saw the "religious and racial fanaticism" of Europe as gaining a foothold in America. As he put it, "Politically, I think, America is not in a good way." The problem as he saw it was that the European "fanatics" were having some influence on the rich and the powerful whose wealth was being used to underwrite ignoble activities of a brutal and unpleasant nature, namely, the formation of groups whose intent was racist. In this letter Loeb named a case in point, "ignorant, stupid, and fanatical . . . Henry Ford . . . no end of mischief can be done by him." Loeb concluded with apparent trepidation, "It is not impossible that that man will gradually buy

28. Loeb to Wolfgang Pauli, 28 June 1920.

29. Loeb to James McKeen Cattell, 24 July 1913.

I thank you for your very kind letter. I feared that you might not altogether approve of what I did. I could not, of course, foresee that the matter would get outside of the club, where it had already been discussed. I suppose newspapers must employ secretaries or janitors to steal papers of this character. I do not, however, think that any great harm has been done. What little there is, is uncomfortable for me rather than for you. About the only thing that they said about you was that you had leanings towards socialism and that is a no more legitimate reason than any other. James McKeen Cattell to Loeb, 21 May 1913.

himself into the presidency of the United States."[30]

Although Loeb admired Albert Einstein he did not share his enthusiasm for Zionism. When Einstein in 1921 invited Loeb to attend a meeting in New York City, he explained that:

> The object of the gathering will be to discuss with a number of gentlemen of standing in the community, the proposed Hebrew University in Jerusalem, and to consider ways and means of organizing in its support the sympathy which is certainly felt toward that scheme in wide circles of American Jewry, both Zionist and non-Zionist.[31]

Loeb was skeptical of both the motives and policies advocated by Zionist leaders such as Chaim Weizmann who was one of the founders and chief ideologists of the Zionist movement. Loeb's views about Zionism were articulated in a letter he wrote to his son Leonard in which he discussed his friend Albert Einstein whom he greatly admired. Loeb described a personal visit by Einstein to Loeb's laboratory, followed by a luncheon for the faculty of the Rockefeller Institute with Einstein as the guest of honor. Although his letter was full of praise and affection for Einstein whom he described as "simple, unassuming, child-like and straight as a human being can be," he was critical of Weizmann, the sponsor for Einstein's visit. Loeb saw Weizmann as an astute, shrewd and manipulative politician. Loeb confided to his son his own suspicion that Weizmann and his fellow Zionists were attempting to use Einstein's good name for their own ends. In his view Zionism was simply another dangerous, narrow nationalism which he abhorred. Loeb endorsed Einstein's interest in the establishment of a university in Jerusalem which might provide a place of study for European Jews, particularly from Poland and Rumania, who have been barred from universities on the Continent. Loeb was in strong sympathy with this objective but remained suspicious of the larger, nationalistic goals of the Zionists.[32]

Loeb, as an internationalist, rejected the Zionist movement's belief that Jews were so threatened in Europe and other Western cultures that they could be safe only in a Jewish state in Palestine. He, like most emancipated Jews prior to the years of the Nazi Holocaust could not see how Jewish nationalism centered in the Middle East could provide a safe haven for Jews. Loeb was one Western intellectual of Jewish ethnic origin who was negatively inclined

30. Loeb to Svante Arrhenius, 8 January 1923.

31. Albert Einstein to Loeb, 9 May 1921.

32. Jacques Loeb to Leonard Loeb, 7 April 1921.

toward the future state of Israel long before it came into existence.

Certainly a vital political issue for Jewish intellectuals of Loeb's generation was that posed by the desire of many Jews of all political persuasions and ethnic and national backgrounds for a place where they could enjoy an independent political and cultural existence. Early Zionist leaders, such as Theodore Herzl and later Chaim Weizmann, had championed the desire of Jews for a return to Palestine and worked hard to get the Balfour Doctrine by the British Foreign Secretary in 1917. However, Loeb, although interested in ending discrimination against the Jews, seemed to be doubtful about helping advance the Zionist cause.

At first, he seemed tentative and uncertain perhaps because he knew little about it; in fact, as late as 1915 he indicated to one of the apparently committed that "next winter he hoped to become better acquainted with your aims and possibilities of Zionism."[33] Richard Gottheil asked Loeb to sign a statement that called for the organization in New York of university men to study and discuss Zionism and the furthering of its aims. This document was signed by a number of prominent Jewish leaders including Louis D. Brandeis, an influential American Jew who was openly Zionist and the first Jew to become a Supreme Court Justice; the core of the statement read as follows:

> This action is being taken in response to the growing demand for such a society. It is largely owing to the fact that there is today no representative club or organization where Zionist topics and theory may be freely discussed and studied that such wide misunderstanding of its aims exists. To obtain a deeper vision of Zionism, in its bearing on the Jewish problem in the world at large, and particularly in America will be the first aim of the proposed society, and to act upon it, when obtained, its hope. It seems proper that those who have enjoyed the advantages of education and study should participate in the solution of virtually the future of the Jews.

Loeb's reply to the request that he become a signatory to the document was this:

> I have just received your kind note of April 25th, signed by Judge Mack, Mr. Brandeis, Mr. Wertheim and yourself. My strong internationalistic attitude makes it impossible for me to sign any appeal in a directly nationalistic enterprise. I am, however, sympathetic to your efforts and should like to receive more information concerning the aims of Zionism.[34]

33. Loeb to Richard J. H. Gottheil, 18 May 1915.

34. Ibid., 5 May 1918.

139

Loeb's reply to Gottheil was well in keeping with the political and ideological tenor of his own beliefs and he remained wary throughout his academic career of efforts to enlist his services in the cause of any "nationalistic enterprise." He did, however, cooperate in aiding Zionists and their fellow-travelers, but he did this primarily by way of advice and consultation never endorsing Zionist aims.[35] Several efforts were made by Zionist leaders to enlist him in the Zionist cause, but Loeb politely resisted their blandishments. In fact, judging from Loeb's correspondence he had been keeping them at arm's length since 1913.[36]

Loeb received various appeals from Jews asking his aid in many causes; some he helped, others he did not. The criteria he often used to make such judgments depended on whether or not the aid could be judged discriminatorily ethnocentric or not. Loeb's criteria for determining whether or not he could support a Jewish cause was summarized as follows:

> I take pleasure in sending you a check for ten dollars to pay for my subscription for 1916 and 1917 to the Jewish Society for the Sanitary Improvement of Palestine. I am afraid that at present the needs there are of a more primitive order than those of sanitary improvement, and I wonder whether anything can be done to improve the lot of those poor suffering people.[37]

However, slightly more than two years earlier, Loeb, when asked for support, told the same individual:

> I regret to say that I am not inclined to sign your appeal, on account of the fact that it emphasizes the Jewish character of

---

35. In a letter to Justice Louis Brandeis, 6 January 1921, Loeb gave the following advice: "I concur in the opinion expressed in a letter sent to you by Dr. Simon Flexner, concerning the desirability of establishing a university in Palestine. It would be wise to begin with the development of the fundamental sciences, e.g. physics and chemistry, for both practical and cultural reasons, and to let the development of other departments of learning follow in the logical sequence. Neither the applied sciences nor the sciences depending upon physics and chemistry, e.g. biology, pathology, and medicine, have any chance if there exist no thoroughly modern and well equipped laboratories of physics and chemistry."

36. On 25 February 1913 Loeb received the following letter from J. L. Magnes who was active in various Jewish causes: "I regret exceedingly that you do not see your way clear to accepting an official trusteeship in the Jewish Agricultural Experiment Station. [In Haifa, Palestine] I am sure that Mr. Aaronsohn will regret it more than anyone when he hear of it on his return to New York from Florida, where he now is. Mr. Aaronsohn will, I know, want to see you before he leaves for Palestine."

37. Loeb to Dr. Harry Friedenwald, 28 June 1917.

the appeal. I think the race problem can only be solved on a broad basis which includes the Negroes, the Japanese, and also the laboring men, in short all the exploited and oppressed. Your appeal is kept in a form which ignores or practically excludes the other problems, and this makes it impossible for me to sign it although I have full sympathy with its aims.[38]

Loeb also had other motives for refusing to support Jewish causes which he felt were either ethnocentric or religious in nature. These motives stemmed from his commitments to secular humanism and scientific materialism. For example, the Intercollegiate Menorah Association which promoted the study and advancement of Jewish culture and ideals, acting through one of its sympathizers, Justice Irving Lehman, asked for Loeb's support. Lehman told him that the Menorah societies had become established on a large number of college and university campuses across the country and provided services to students of "a very high spiritual value." The societies were planning a convention in New York with the students from across the country in attendance and Lehman asked Loeb to participate in welcoming and honoring the students and providing "the recognition they deserve."[39] Loeb's answer was brief, to the point, and consistent with his atheistic materialism:

Please accept my thanks for your invitation to join in a meeting of the Menorah Societies. While I can well understand the high motives which guide you in fostering the aims of this organization, I regret to say that the work to which my life has been devoted has been in opposition to the traditions of romanticism.[40]

Loeb's efforts to keep Jewish religious groups at bay were congruent with his internationalism, atheism and materialist philosophy; his negative attitudes toward early Zionism should not be viewed as unusual. Indeed, many Jewish intellectuals of his time were skeptical both of the ideology and the aims of the Zionist movement. However, it should be kept in mind that the programmatics and doctrine of Zionism were viewed differently before the Holocaust than after. Since Loeb did not live to see the destruction of European Jewry, it is impossible to say how he might have reacted to later Zionism.

38. Ibid., 5 May 1915.

39. Justice Irving Lehman to Loeb, 17 Dec. 1917.

40. Loeb to Justice Irving Lehman, 24 Dec. 1917.

CHAPTER SEVEN
THE GREAT DISILLUSIONMENT:
THE AFTERMATH OF WAR

———◆———

THE POSTWAR BLUES

Loeb became seriously depressed by World War I and never fully
recovered from it, as is evident in his correspondence; the
optimism and hope for international harmony that were part of
the Victorian Era which nurtured him were shattered. This
combined with the dismal economic and cultural/political
environment of the postwar period made him acutely unhappy at
times. It is easy to document this because he wrote and talked
about it on many occasions. Although at times Loeb was able to
see some hope for the future, he tended to be strongly pessimistic,
a pessimism that was apparently shared and reinforced by his wife
Anne. World events combined with bouts of ill health made their
last years at times less than happy ones. Loeb commented in his
correspondence that "I have stopped reading the newspapers, and
I am trying to preserve at least my scientific optimism."[1] To
another European acquaintance he wrote in 1920 that in his own
view world conditions had failed to improve in the two years since
the end of the great conflict in Europe. In fact he seems to suggest
that the very activities involved in the prosecution of the war, such
as training young men in what Loeb sarcastically refers to as "the
gentle art of bayoneting," has put the world on a path leading to
a "return to the Dark Ages." He points to the fact that Albert

---

1. Loeb to Richard Goldschmidt, 16 February 1921. The toll taken by the War on
Loeb and his family was apparently considerable. In his own words:

   The war has been a terrible burden on us and it is needless to say that both Anne
   and I have suffered a good deal. Our oldest son, Leonard, was in France with the
   anti-aircraft service, but he is back now and has a National Research Fellowship
   in Physics and is working in Chicago. After the war he was for some time with
   Professor Rutherford in Manchester and did what I think is a good piece of
   work. Our second boy, Robert, has finished his medical study and is a intern in
   the Massachusetts General Hospital in Boston. He was about ready to go to
   France at the time of the armistice but remained here. Our youngest child,
   Anne, is now seventeen years old and in school.—Anne suffered from the
   influenza which affected her heart and has not been quite well since.

   Loeb to [his uncle] Harry Bresslau, 29 October 1919.

Einstein was forced to leave Berlin as simply more evidence of the decline of the civilized order.[2]

In a similar vein, in another letter written just two months later, Loeb declares again his deep state of depression, brought about not only by the residue of the war per se, but also by the very nature of the peace in postwar Europe. He repeatedly reflects on his belief that the war and its aftermath have produced in humanity a condition which he labels as "insane." Loeb states, "While animals are kept in a definite line of conduct by their simple tropisms, the natural tropisms of human beings can be diversified by phrases and . . . thus be rendered abnormal or insane . . . [from which] they will never be able to return."[3] This theme, the insanity caused by the conflict, is one that Loeb will return to time and again in the post–war years.

Not long before he died, Loeb wrote to the French scientist Georges Bohn in Paris. It was now five years after World War I, yet he returns again to his perception that the world is returning to "the Dark Ages," although his perception of decline is now focused more on the Continent than the world at large. Loeb's perception is that conditions in Europe can only lead to a more dismal and terrible future (events in Germany ten brief years later were to prove him correct). He once again described himself as having totally withdrawn into his work. (His continued involvement in various causes and projects, as we have tried to highlight them, do not correspond with this self-portrait.) The one island of light in an otherwise dark and gloomy world, as he saw it, was in the sciences, and particularly in the areas of chemistry and physics. He seemed a little less certain of biology, but was hopeful. He argued that when the world was ready for a return to sanity, the sciences would lead the way. But for the time being he was deeply pessimistic when he said just months before his death, "I never dreamed that at the end of my life I should have to abandon all hope of any benefit to humanity through my work, and simply work in isolation trying to forget the condition of the world surrounding me."[4] The pathos with which this last statement reeks is not a measure of Loeb's self-pity; rather, it is a commentary on what world affairs and, perhaps, ill-health can do to a brilliant, idealistic and rapidly aging scientist.

---

2. Loeb to Richard Beutner, 18 October 1920.

3. Loeb to Madame Drzewina and Georges Bohn, 15 December 1920.

4. Loeb to Georges Bohn, 25 May 1923.

COMMENTARY ON POLITICAL AND ECONOMIC AFFAIRS

That Loeb was always an interested observer and sometimes perceptive critic of both domestic and international affairs is abundantly evident in his correspondence both with American and European friends and scientists. Few significant events transpired anywhere in the Western world that did not catch his eye. This appears to have been consistently true after his emigration to the United States in 1891; however, since little correspondence from the period prior to his emigration has survived, it is impossible to say if the young Loeb shared these interests although it seems likely.

In 1919 the radical Bela Kun and his Marxist followers seized power in Hungary and attempted to establish a Soviet regime similar to the one newly installed in Russia; abortive efforts to collectivize agricultural resources and communize the rest of the political economy failed and the regime collapsed after a few months in power. Its collapse was followed by a seizure of power by the extreme right which ushered in a two decade long dictatorship by the Admiral Horthy regime which was accompanied by vicious reprisals and political repression. Loeb was both a fascinated and horrified observer of these events and wrote to a scientific colleague in Budapest that the brutal tactics of the Hungarian government were having an extremely negative effect on world public opinion. In this letter Loeb suggests, perhaps naively, that if the reactionary elements of the Hungarian government understood the perception of their behavior "in the eyes of the civilized world, I think they would come to their senses."[5]

Loeb was unusually pessimistic in his analyses of both domestic and international affairs after the War started in the summer of 1914. Although he sometimes praised the values and policies of President Wilson, he actually had a profound distrust of almost all political leaders who wielded power. Early in 1916, before U. S. entry into the War, he told his German uncle that the decisions of the Wilson government concerning matters both foreign and domestic were being dictated by political considerations. Loeb reported that American public opinion toward Germany, in light of recent events such as the invasion of Belgium and the sinking of the Lusitania, had become progressively more negative, and he attributed this shift, at least in part, to his perception that "Americans are very emotional and superficial." Wilson was being forced by political considerations to respond to this shift in public opinion, Loeb observed, and thus he has taken up the cause of "war

---

5. Loeb to A. Koranyi, 13 January 1921.

preparedness" in the face of purported military threats from Germany and Japan. Warming to his topic, Loeb went on to decry various Wilson political appointments which Loeb perceived as being motivated by the most base of political objectives. However, he showed himself to be a pragmatist when he turned his attention to the alternatives in the upcoming elections. Loeb declared, "On the other hand, Roosevelt is a megalomaniac, who has only one desire, namely to remain in the White House perpetually, and if possible become a dictator." Loeb concluded on a familiar theme "banking interests, big business . . . the munition industry, run a country . . . politicians obey their orders. I think this is the same here and in Europe."[6] Loeb was clearly disgusted with either alternative, Wilson or Roosevelt, but he did show a special disappointment with Wilson since the latter had come from an academic background, was a former university president, and "ought to know better," (the latter comment was actually a reference to Wilson's appointment of a veterinarian to the Geodetic Survey). In this letter Loeb thus stressed several of his favorite themes: the first was the unprincipled behavior of politicians; the second, their intervention for political gain in institutions and processes they did not understand; and the third, the way in which corporate interests were able to manipulate them in ways detrimental to the interests of the common man.

In retrospect and in spite of Loeb's avowed "pacifism," he seems to have viewed the War and its consequences as an immense evil, but by late 1919 he had also come to believe that it had some positive results. This was his analysis in a letter he wrote to his German aunt and uncle, in which he declared that the terrible postwar misery which the world was experiencing was ultimately brought about by the actions of the Hohenzollerns and the Habsburgs who initiated the conflict. American entry into the war had as its goal the destruction of the "military aristocracy" in central Europe;

---

6. Loeb to Harry Bresslau, 27 January 1916. The reader also gets this progress report on Loeb's family followed by reflections on the present discontents. "My two boys were with us during the Christmas vacation. My eldest boy, Leonard, is about to get his doctor's degree in physics at the University of Chicago, and will probably have a position next year in California. My second boy is studying medicine in Harvard, and my little girl is very much interested in art and very averse to any effort at learning. Anne is tolerably well but the war has discouraged her completely. It is hard for you to realize to what extent this war has broken the hopefulness and courage of reformers of all kinds. We all realize that, after all, the middle ages are not yet a matter of the past and that nothing matters very much except the one thing, science, which is bound to progress in spite of the shortcomings of all its individual contributors. In ten thousand years we may possibly have what may be termed civilization."

furthermore, the harsh postwar peace conditions demanded by the French were aimed at preventing its resurgence. Loeb predicted that if there were a subsequent resurgence of German militarism, world reaction could threaten the very existence of Germany. The latter view was particularly prescient on Loeb's part, given that the division of Germany in 1945 into two quite separate portions was to persist for almost forty-five years. Loeb described American public opinion as holding the view that U.S. participation in the war was necessary in order to remove militaristic forces from central Europe, but that it was also important for this country to avoid further entanglements in European affairs.[7]

On many occasions Loeb was asked for help in obtaining academic or other positions for German scientists whose situation after the War was apparently very bad. Mostly, Loeb told these men in his correspondence with them that there was little that he could do to help them, at least in the immediate future, because of the persistence of strong anti-German feelings in America. The situation was made even worse by the post-war downturn in the economy. In a letter to one supplicant, Loeb made it clear that while conditions may be better outside of Germany they were by no means ideal. Economic conditions had reduced scientific employment opportunities in industry to nil. Furthermore, academic opportunities in universities were blocked for Germans due to a residue of antipathy toward citizens of the former Central Powers: "I cannot say that they feel any hatred but it is obviously not considered good form to have Germans around." Loeb clearly suggested that this resentment toward newly arrived Germans was more pronounced in academic circles than elsewhere in society. In Loeb's words "time will change that but I am afraid scientific circles are more conservative than the rest."[8]

It is interesting to note that Loeb rarely lost sight of his own philosophical and epistemological commitments even when discussing topics that at first glance might seem quite far removed from the arena of scholarship. It is also significant that his ideological and doctrinal opponents would not let him forget them either as a 1917 letter to a French scientific colleague, Maurice Caullery, demonstrates. Loeb had written a defense of the mechanistic theoretical framework in which he attempted to refute the oft-repeated claim that it was the mechanistic approach that was the precipitatory cause of wars. In a subsequent communication Caullery had pointed out that Loeb had failed to adequately deal with the fact that Germany and Austria had started the war. Loeb replied, rather

---

7. Loeb to Harry Bresslau, 29 October 1919.

8. Loeb to Reinhard Beutner, 28 November 1921.

testily, that "it was not my intention to write a book about the war . . . only to defend mechanists against the reproach . . . that it is mechanism that makes for wars."[9] Apparently, Loeb was here responding to those religionists who had attempted to blame the War on the spread of mechanistic and materialist doctrine of the sort that he preached.

Loeb may not have become a cynic in the aftermath of the World War, but at times his case of the "postwar blues" was acute. In a 1921 letter to a friend, Loeb proposes that a millennium may pass before humans advance to a "happy state of wisdom . . .by that time," he reflects, "the human monkeys may have annihilated each other completely." This is not the only occasion on which Loeb emphasizes man's close association with other primates—in a clearly derogatory manner. It seems yet another reflection of the pessimism that afflicted him with the onset of the war. He goes on to suggest that relief from such a condition is to be found only in the laboratory "or in some other form of cloistral existence."[10]

Loeb sometimes made penetrating comments about contemporary cultural events and on one occasion he analyzed an influential play in these words:

> It is perhaps not generally realized that in the manufacturing of racial prejudice, especially in its violent and noisy form, the moral imbecile and that type of romanticist who may be better designated as semi-paranoid have had a prominent share. . . . The writer does not know the author of the play "The Birth of a Nation" and hence cannot express any judgment as to his mental or moral condition. "The Birth of a Nation" can in the writer's opinion, however, be best characterized as a display of homicidal paranoia with a special grievance against the Negro. The sad and dangerous part is that this homicidal paranoia seemed also to take possession, temporarily at least, of part of the audience. To call this diabolic appeal to race hatred and this display of scenes of murder "The Birth of a Nation" is the worst insult that has ever been heaped upon this country. The writer is no great believer in censorship and he feels that any pressure from without towards suppressing the play will only result in greater advertisement for it. Would it not be best to appeal to the common sense and the decency of the theatrical people to unite against performances of this kind in the future and to quietly drop "The Birth of a Nation" for the present?[11]

9. Loeb to Maurice Caullery, 26 June 1917.

10. Loeb to E. Burnet, 2 May 1921.

11. Loeb to J. E. Spingarn, 17 March 1915.

Even a casual reading of Loeb's correspondence during the War makes a veritable chronicle not only of what is occurring both militarily and diplomatically, but also of Loeb's own evolving views toward the conflagration that continuously threatened to spread and engulf his adopted country. In a 1915 letter to his friend Wolfgang Ewald, Loeb makes clear again his position that the war continues because it generates immense profits or as he puts it "God Profit dictates that the war must be maintained and if profits are not big enough then our country must go to war with Germany too." Because of the vast profits that were being generated in the United States without the problems of direct involvement, Loeb surmised that the "moneyed powers" would be so accustomed to the flow of riches that America would become the cause, the "chief fomenter" of wars in the future. By this time Loeb saw as inevitable the eventual involvement of this country in the war. He felt that the majority of Americans expected it and that the "capitalistic newspapers" encouraged it. He concluded, "I do not think that America differs so much in this respect from Europe, only in Europe the making of profits out of a war is confined to certain privileged classes and hence is not so general as in America."[12]

Loeb repeatedly stated his belief that the armaments industry and the desire for profits were behind the war preparedness movement in the United States. Militarism was becoming rampant and sooner rather than later the American armed forces would be sent overseas. The enthusiasm of war fever had grown to such a pitch that Loeb declared he was no longer able to read the paper. He deplored what he regarded as "a general condition of prostitution." Wilson had abandoned his earlier peace position, Loeb concluded, and now argued in favor of armaments and "preparedness." However, when he compared Wilson with Roosevelt as a potential occupier of the White House, Loeb considered Wilson "a blessing."[13]

At this point, Loeb was sticking by his pacifist ideals and his analysis was consistent with them. He recognized that Secretary of State William Jennings Bryan had a strong pacifist streak for which he admired him. He was also aware that Wilson had a more conciliatory diplomatic stance than the bellicose Theodore Roosevelt, an early advocate of interventionism whose rhetoric, Loeb believed, verged on the blood-thirsty and the hysterical. Loeb's analysis was thus a penetrating blend of moral idealism and political realism. But he was ultimately to become very disillusioned with Woodrow Wilson and, at

---

12. Loeb to Wolfgang F. Ewald, 29 July 1915.

13. Loeb to William Roux, 5 October 1915.

times, with humanity; this disillusionment, of course, coincided with the onset of the postwar blues. Loeb described Wilson as "either hopelessly incompetent or hopelessly hypocritical" and hoped that the day would come when politicians such as Wilson would be seen to have made a calamity of the post-war situation. In an interesting use of words, Loeb said that "perhaps the human simians will recognize what men like Wilson . . . have done."[14] Once again he uses the link to sub-human primates; perhaps he is suggesting that Darwin was wrong, not in proposing our link to the apes, but in proposing we have descended very far at all. Loeb was thus knowledgeable enough about the international situation to recognize larger trends as they began to evolve. He was most unhappy about the turn of events in the United States and Europe and sensitive enough to realize that the postwar trends were already in the direction of reaction, repression and authoritarianism.

Loeb's attitude toward Wilson did not improve after the middle years of the War. Nevertheless, he was politically shrewd enough to realize that the overwhelming defeat of the Wilsonian Democratic ticket of James M. Cox and Franklin D. Roosevelt in 1920 had only made things worse from the viewpoint of intellectuals of his own ideological stripe. He saw the shift from Woodrow Wilson to Warren Harding as a change that foretold the advent of an era of reactionary conservatism. As he put it, "the human race, I think, is still essentially composed of monkeys whose natural habitat is the jungle, and the only civilized part in that jungle is the realm of exact science." Once again we see Loeb's reference to the problems of the world and the promise of the experimental laboratory. Of course, once again, his reference is to man as a monkey.[15]

Loeb was no admirer of monarchy or aristocracy in any form. His feelings toward the Russian monarchy were particularly negative. He described Czar Nicholas II (1894-1917) as being of marginal mental capacity, using the terms "low mentality" and "semi-idiotic," a condition which he ascribed to heredity. Loeb concluded with a particularly damning statement, "but whatever the cause may be, the fact remains that the programs in Russia are instigated by a morally and intellectually defective human being who unfortunately has supreme power over more than a hundred million people."[16] It is noteworthy here that the biologist Loeb was using his knowledge of genetics to explain the moral character and

14. Loeb to Aristide Rieffel, 9 August 1919.

15. Loeb to Harry Bresslau, 21 February 1921.

16. Loeb to J. E. Spingarn, 17 March 1915.

political behavior of the Russian ruler whose government not only encouraged vicious anti-Semitism, but bore much responsibility for the massive bloodletting that was occurring.

Loeb's initial reaction to the Bolshevik Revolution was favorable, although he was soon to become disillusioned with Soviet Communism.

> The Bolsheviks are the saviors of civilization and are setting an example such as the world has not seen since the French revolution. Their informing the Persian Government that as far as Russia is concerned the treaty between Russia and England concerning the division of Persia is null and void, and that Russia will insist upon the full freedom of Persia is wonderful. The Germans are robbers, and I think the Italian and English governmental classes, and perhaps the French capitalistic class too, are not very much better. Capitalistic imperialism and exploitation is the game all over.[17]

It is significant to note that by 1918 when Loeb wrote these comments, he had become disillusioned with almost all existing regimes except the most radical and he was soon to become quite skeptical about the new regime in Russia on account of its repression and bloody excesses.

Conclusion

Although, unlike some Western radicals, Loeb was not obsessed with events in Russia, he was very interested in Soviet Communism in its initial stages; his skepticism about the beneficence of Bolshevism developed relatively early and even though he did not live to see Stalinism with both its vast apparatus of oppression and enormous industrial growth, he cannot be accused of naiveté. He wrote to a European colleague roughly at the time Lenin introduced the New Economic Plan to this effect:

> I fully agree with you about the consequences of the peace though I am not quite certain that the Russian revolution has not done as much harm in one way as it has done good in the other. It seems that when human beings get into power they are bound to lose their heads, and I am afraid the proletarian when drunk with power is no better than the capitalist in the same condition. I have given up taking much interest in the affairs of

17. Loeb to Hardolph Wasteneys, 2 February 1918.

18. Loeb to E. Burnet, 2 May 1921.

the world since they are too depressing and since humanity is bound to repeat the same blunders until one day quantitative science has been developed to such a degree and has permeated the masses so universally that all those terrible blunders we are noticing today can be avoided.[18]

Thus, even the monumental upheaval in Russia, in Loeb's view, came to no good end, at least none that he could support with conviction or conscience. It only added to his disillusionment with the postwar trends and compounded his pessimism regarding the future.

It has been suggested by Phillip Pauly that Loeb was a mainstay in the development of the "engineering ideal" in biology which once inspired the latter to comment that:

> It was perhaps not the least important of Darwin's services to science that the boldness of his conceptions gave to the experimental biologist courage to enter upon the attempt of controlling at will the life phenomena of animals, and of bringing about effects which cannot be expected in nature.[19]

Perhaps Loeb's postwar disillusionment and depression can be traced ultimately not only to his ill-health and that of his wife, but also to the frustration, if not the collapse, of his dreams for social control and political reconstruction. It is evident that his social philosophy and political activism was rooted in the engineering ideal in biology and, in fact, was largely its extension into human affairs. His laboratory experiments with the tropismatic responses of animals led him to the belief that a more advanced behavioral technology could be developed and applied to the process of social change both to check adult pathologies and to mold desirable traits and habits in the young.

It is true, of course, that more recent proponents of behavioral technologies a la operant conditioning such as Burrhus Frederick Skinner have been charged with harboring totalitarian aspirations and utopian dreams and of believing that radical environmental conditioning is not really a betrayal of human freedom and dignity. Had Loeb's views on social engineering been more widely publicized and had he written utopian novels like *Walden Two* he would, no doubt, have been mistakenly subjected to the same scathing criticism. It appears, however, that academic political, and social philosophers and journalists were mostly unaware of his existence or, if they were aware, knew little or nothing of his qualified espousal of the engineering ideal in biology and human affairs.

---

19. Loeb, *The Mechanistic Conception of Life*, p. 195.

CHAPTER EIGHT
EPILOGUE: EPISTEMOLOGY, SOCIAL CONTROL AND POLITICAL ACTIVISM

INTRODUCTION

Peter Kuznick has argued that by the 1930s the American and British scientific communities had identified four main problems confronting scientists in the international community. These were problems that Loeb himself had identified earlier and according to Kuznick they included:

> (1) economic insecurity resulting from years of expensive education, low salaries, high unemployment, and infrequent pensions; (2) apprehension about the "misapplication of scientific discovery and the inefficiency with which the benefits of scientific knowledge and invention are made available to the general public"; (3) interference with scientific research in the form of funding cuts and curbs on freedom of speech; and (4) "a marked tendency to make use of pseudo-scientific ideas to excuse war and to attack reason and democracy."[1]

Years earlier, Loeb had expressed concern over the ideological rigidity and myopia of government officials; he had recognized the danger of politicians and bureaucrats interfering with the autonomy of scientific inquiry and imposing doctrinal straitjackets on American and European scientists. The potential danger of ideologically dictated science which was to reach its zenith under the Nazi and Stalinist regimes had counterparts in miniature during Loeb's career in the form of sporadic interference with funding of "objectionable" projects or the removal of scientists from official positions for political reasons. He preferred that scientists be funded on the basis of the merit of their research as judged by competent scientists on scientific grounds rather than by narrowly political or ideological criteria; but he also recognized that as government expanded its funding, it might yield to the temptation

---

1. Peter J. Kuznick, *Beyond the Laboratory: Scientists as Political Activists in 1930s America* (Chicago: University of Chicago Press, 1987), p. 228.

to unnecessarily meddle in the affairs of science. He had ample opportunity to observe the way corporate money was used to control the development of both pure and applied science and became increasingly sensitive to the imposition of either government or corporate constraints on the autonomy of the scientific community.

The moral and philosophical basis for Loeb's political and social activism rested in part on his belief that scientists should organize or even prod their colleagues toward progressive social and political action. Expressions of the new social activism among scientists, as Kuznick has shown,[2] were to become much more common in the 1930s than the early decades of the twentieth century. Unlike his counterparts a decade or so after his death in 1924, Loeb rarely had to defend science against charges that its findings were responsible for militarism, mass murder, and other claims coming from inside and outside the scientific community to the effect that its accomplishments were used for socially destructive purposes. Nevertheless, Loeb's commitment to scientific method brought him continuously into conflict with the existing culture and socioeconomic system in the United States. His strenuous efforts to rally progressives fell basically on that portion of the scientific community that was interested in or actively involved with reform. Indeed, it may safely be claimed that he wasted little time on those individuals and groups that he regarded as too morally and intellectually primitive to merit his attention; before pessimism and fatalism began to overtake him in the postwar period, he did hope to inculcate a greater sense of social conscience and social responsibility in other liberal-minded intellectuals, although needless to say he did not suffer fools gladly. Still, Loeb had little to say by way of criticizing science for disavowing responsibility for the uses that society made of its discoveries. He had disdain for those motivated by personal financial gain as their main motive for undertaking scientific research, yet he did not much concern himself about the role played by science and scientists in providing society with novel ideas and tools utilizable for socially destructive purposes. Probably, he felt that the main responsibility for how science was used was more corporate and governmental than individual, although he did not absolve the scientific community of the larger social consequences of their work.

Loeb realized that scientists often claimed to be ethically neutral and that this attitude on the part of scientists posed some

2. Ibid., p. 86.

risk to society. Although they might avoid political involvement, their research often had unavoidable, if indirect, social and political effects.[3] The prevailing norms within the scientific community had not yet shifted to a demand on the part of scientists for an ethic of social concern and responsibility, but Loeb's view was clearly a harbinger of things to come during the depression decade and the war that followed it.

What distinguished Loeb from many of his scientific contemporaries was his claim that the kind of society that could make the best use of science was more important than whether science could be adjusted to the demands of society. What he proposed was a progressive approach to be sure, but not one so radical that it would alienate socially-minded liberal scientists. But given the number of apolitical and politically conservative scientists with whom he had to interact, it was not surprising that he sometimes became frustrated. While he exposed pseudo-scientific theories when they were used as a rationale in defense of militarism, anti-labor, anti-democratic and socially destructive policies, he found to his chagrin that an important segment within the scientific community supported, or acquiesced in, these policies. For this and other reasons such as the possibility of increased centralization of control which he feared, he was skeptical of the possibility of creating a unifying body, that is, an umbrella organization for all progressive-minded scientists that would ally itself with liberal nonscientific organizations to secure a wider application of science and the understanding of scientific method for the welfare of society. Instead, he favored working with

---

3. E. G. Boring has written that:

Lloyd Morgan's caution was re-enforced by Loeb's theory of the tropism, which was offered to the world at the same time. Loeb had little difficulty in convincing the readers of his paper that plants and protozoa are virtually Cartesian automata in their responses to stimulation. If tropistic action is determined entirely by physicochemical forces, it may therefore be supposed to be independent of volition or reason. No more than Descartes did Loeb think, however, that men are mere automata, governed only by unconscious tropisms. He sought, rather, to establish the point in the evolutionary scale at which consciousness emerges, and concluded that the existence of associative memory, the ability of an organism to profit by experience, demonstrates the emergence of mind. Since the higher vertebrates obviously possess associative memory, the effect of Loeb's argument was to preserve a dualism, but to shift the critical point of separation lower down in the evolutionary scale. Men and dogs are conscious, protozoa and plants are not. Such a view supports the Darwinian theory because it fills in the "missing link" between man and the animals.

E. G. Boring, "The Influence of Evolutionary Theory Upon American Psychological Thought" in *Evolutionary Thought in America*, (ed.) Stow Persons (New York: Archon Books, 1968), pp. 285-86.

organizations that were specifically issue or task-oriented rather than all-encompassing in terms of their programmatic and doctrinal outlook.

Loeb, although he often inveighed against the use of scientific method and findings for political and scientific objectives with which he disagreed, nevertheless realized that scientific method could be used to justify more conservative political and moral positions. Even though he maintained that his own radicalism emanated naturally from the scientific *weltanschauung*, he recognized that to many within the scientific community the scientific method favored political moderation as opposed to any large-scale social engineering or experimentation. He often criticized other scientists, nevertheless, for ignoring scientific method when they formulated their own social and political philosophies. He knew, even when his own rhetoric belied it, the difficulty of subjecting all knowledge, especially political and cultural hypotheses, to vigorous testing and proof. Indeed, his own narrow view of science with its fixation on quantitative method would make impossible the conversion of what passed for social studies into social science. At times he came dangerously close, if he did not actually embrace, a position of scientistic fundamentalism for it was not until late in life that his faith in the beneficence of science was disturbed. Even then he apparently believed that in the long run science would triumph over atavistic and reactionary cultural views and social practices.

Loeb was aware that the scientific community was already quite heterogeneous in terms of its ethnic, religious and socioeconomic composition and this tended to be the prime determinant of the political and social philosophies most commonly held within it: individual views of scientific method and the findings of science were thus secondary to the social and cultural prisms through which scientific knowledge was interpreted. Thus adherence to the scientific method with its self-reflective focus on logic and verification was only one element in determining political and moral values. Often it was not the most important one as Loeb himself acknowledged when he continuously harped on the way religious beliefs insidiously infected the scientific work of his peers.

Until the Great War erupted, Loeb hoped to attract a broad coalition of politically progressive scientists to the many causes he favored, so he tended to avoid policies and rhetoric that would unnecessarily antagonize those more conservative than himself. But he realized that events in the early 1920s reinforced the identification of many such scientists with the dominant institutional structures. Mostly corporate power and the money of

156

capitalists controlled the growth of science outside universities through the financing of industrial research laboratories, research institutes, and philanthropic foundations including the Rockefeller Institute, itself, which employed Loeb; and academe was certainly not immune to the blandishment and support of the American upperclass. Loeb could only resent that many "leaders" of science themselves epitomized political and social orthodoxy which made them acceptable to people with money even though their work might be devoid of scientific merit or novelty.

Thus it seems fair to say that despite or perhaps, in part, because of his Old World, that is European background and his New World experiences and cultural indoctrination, Loeb made considerable progress in defining for himself, at least, an organically American radicalism; a "critical theory" so to speak which was congruent with egalitarian views of democracy and social justice while maintaining a belief in material abundance rooted in scientific and technological advance. And yet, despite his occasional protests to the contrary, Loeb never seems to have felt quite at home here, perhaps because of the cultural elitism bred in him by his Old World education and residence in such hotbeds of European culture as Berlin.

LOEB AND THE AMERICAN IDEOLOGY OF NATIONAL SCIENCE

Historian of science Ronald Tobey has argued that leading scientists were motivated to seek a public consensus on an ideology of "national science" in the 1920s and that "national science" had two related meanings. As he put it:

> It refers to the centralized administration of nongovernmental scientific activity by a private agency of the kind that developed during the First World War for war-related research. It refers also to the articulated, explicit relevance of the values of professional science to the values of nonscientists, whether the latter be the officially sponsored ideals of the federal government in the First World War or the economic and political values which the scientists thought the general public held in the 1920s.[4]

Although Loeb was certainly a leading scientist of the day, he remained an outsider, as he had been all of his life, when it came to

---

4. Ronald C. Tobey, *The American Ideology of National Science*, 1919-1930 (Pittsburgh: University of Pittsburgh Press, 1971), p. XII.

the promotion or institutionalization of an ideology of national science. He distrusted the motives of several of the would-be "centralizers" of science, was disillusioned with the national goals of the American political leadership, and skeptical whether much good could come from federally funded research, if government control accompanied it. At the same time he was well aware of the pitfalls of corporate and commercial control as scientists sought to avoid the dangers of conservatism while accommodating themselves to the values of big-business donors. In the final analysis, Loeb did not want to alter the professional role of scientists by tying them to either government or corporate interests.

Loeb was often dismayed but not surprised by public ignorance of current development in science; in part this was because his main focus was on "pure science" not on applied research. While other "progressives" focused on the concept of the expert as exemplified in scientific management, scientific government and professional engineering, he tended as he aged, to bury himself more and more in the claim that pure science without immediate utilitarian aims was the key to social value. While some liberal scientists and laymen tried to relate the values of science to those of American culture, Loeb, in a depressed state of mind from the postwar blues, seemed to relinquish such aspirations. He came to feel that it would be a very long time before the common man could accommodate himself to the ethos of modern science.

Loeb was always somewhat vague as to what the relationships were between the values of science and those of political reform, social engineering and muckraking journalism. He remained committed to the ideology of science with its fundamental proposition "that scientific ideas conceived within the framework of theories about the nature of the physical world were [should be] the primary causes of cultural change."[5] Yet as he rapidly aged after the Great War, he seemed to put the millennium of science off for a long time to come for its progressive thrust had been misdirected by the institutional resurgence of racism, class interest and dogmatic religious belief.

Loeb clearly believed that scientific ideas could initiate qualitative, historical change, yet he failed to understand or at least he failed to specify the conditions under which this might occur. Like other alert and committed scientists of his time he more or less continuously tried to define the values of science for the American public; he attempted valiantly to relate scientific values to other cultural values especially political ones, and, while he tried to relate

5. Ibid., p. 74.

scientific knowledge to shared social goals, he often found to his dismay that these goals, if they could be identified at all, were not to his liking. Racism, entrenched class privilege, and religious superstition were endemic to American society and Loeb became pessimistic about defeating them, at least in the short run. He probably never relinquished hope of overcoming the alienation of the laity from science through inculcation of the method and values of science, but in old age he was decidedly more pessimistic about such a possibility than he had been earlier. Perhaps his old friend Thorstein Veblen had finally succeeded in indoctrinating him with his ideas of cultural lag and institutional resistance to change; or more likely, he was finally forced to the realization that several of his prime values were not widely enough shared in the society he had adopted to matter politically.

Unlike many other scientists of the Progressive Era, roughly 1901-1917, Loeb did not believe that democracy could be a substitute for science because it made experimentation unnecessary. On the contrary the scientific method as social method relied not only on experimentation, but also on a scientism deeply rooted in the metaphysics, epistemology and ontology of reductionistic materialism. This position was much more radical than those held by most of his contemporaries and although he certainly held to the tenets of democratic theory-political equality, majority rule and minority rights—he believed, probably correctly, that democracy as he interpreted it would flourish best in a scientifically sanitized social order devoid of racism, superstition and class privilege.

Although a casual observer might view Loeb's theoretical system, that is, his mechanistic materialism as allowing little role for ideational autonomy and volition, he, nevertheless, believed ideas had a primary and creative role in human interaction with the natural and social environment. As contradictory as this may seem, it is explicable within his paradigm because of the role that associative imagery plays in giving the individual some choice as regards their own beliefs and course of action. Loeb's sometimes caustic criticism of the moral and political inertia and conservatism of other scientists would be difficult to square with his own theoretical system if they had no choice as to what to believe or whether to engage in social activism. Yet Ronald Tobey writes that:

> It had been a common criticism, especially during the struggle over evolutionary theory, that science promoted philosophical materialism which in turn dried up the human spirit. Certainly,

this criticism was true of the nineteenth-century tendency toward physicalism in, for example, the biological work of Jacques Loeb. Though the national scientists like [Physicist Robert] Millikan were reluctant to accept the scientific revolution wrought by the theories of relativity, they did recognize that this revolution had demolished nineteenth-century scientific materialism. Relativity and quantum theories had described the existence of irreducible, qualitatively distinct levels of physical reality. The theories thereby thwarted the effort of materialists to reduce all phenomena, including human experience and consciousness, to the motions of atoms. Without necessarily endorsing the other philosophical implication of the new physics, the national scientists would point out that materialism no longer threatened man's spiritual life.[6]

Tobey also writes that:

American liberalism has considered itself scientific since the progressive era, but this scientific character has sprung from social science, scientific management, and rational engineering, not from the physical sciences with which the scientific method originated. The struggle of the scientists in the 1920s to regain possession of the symbols of science and the scientific method represented their awareness that the values and method of pure science had to have a naturally sanctioned connection to the social values of democracy if the two cultures were to have a deep unity. Their failure was due to the new physics which destroyed the classical vision of revelatory science, to the conservative pressures of a disintegrating progressivism, and to industrial capitalism in the 1920s. The separation of the two cultures can never be overcome if scientists think in terms of public relations or of education to values which the struggle of the 1920s showed not to be within the democratic consensus.[7]

Loeb's view, of course, was that science had only begun to penetrate the ethos of liberalism and that, in any case, liberalism itself, was not well assimilated into popular culture.

But Tobey also comments in a manner that Loeb might have agreed with:

That an intellectual activity over three hundred years old should now have an "identity crisis" reveals the depth of pure science's ideological problem in American democracy. America

---

6. Ibid., p. 181.

7. Ibid., p. 231.

has not provided the symbols, tasks, or institutions which could establish the place of pure science within the culture. Consequently, pure science must constantly redefine itself both to be distinguished and to be eligible for the money which government grants to certain scientific activities.[8]

Ultimately, another severe political problem was to arise which Loeb never adequately acknowledged, the problem of democratic control over technical experts and scientists. Philosopher James Campbell poses the problem this way:

> If we allow for the possibility of legitimate and illegitimate persuasion in society, we still have the practical problem of deciding whether particular instances of persuasion are manipulative or beneficial. Defining manipulation, with C. Wright Mills, as the secretive use of unauthorized power, we would have to admit that experts certainly have the capacity of manipulation and have often exercised it. However, the fault here seems to lie not with Dewey's suggestion that we establish a role for experts, for we could not live as we do today without them. The fault is ours: it lies in our failure to maintain critical control over our experts. Although we recognize with Dewey that no individual or group of individuals "is wise enough or good enough to rule others without their consent," we have been all too willing to consent to whatever the experts tell us. We have all too often forgotten that expertise results not from intellectual superiority, and still less from moral preeminence, but from a publicly verifiable method. We have paid dearly for this failure, and until we begin to control our experts we will continue to pay.[9]

Loeb knew that no industrial culture, whether governed "democratically" or not, could flourish without large numbers of competent technical specialists and scientists to sustain it. Yet he was not given to speculating as to how these groups could contribute to the making of policy without usurping the control function itself. He may have been guilty of hubris by ignoring the potential threat experts pose to democracy, but in his own lifetime (1859-1924), technical and scientific elites encroached less on the social and political decision-making processes than they do today.

---

8. Ibid., p. 232.

9. James Campbell, *The Community Reconstructs: The Meaning of Pragmatic Social Thought* (Urbana: University of Illinois Press, 1992), p. 52.

CONCLUSION

Loeb's specific role in the history of science and his larger role in American intellectual history may best be understood as the point of convergence of three streams of thought. These are (1) philosophical materialism of the mechanistic-reductionist variety, (2) biology understood from the engineering point of view with obvious implications for social control and, (3) politico-social activist doctrine with all this suggests for reconstruction of the human order. Loeb understood the implications of these converging streams of thought for the future of humanity; indeed, he pinned his hopes on them only to become increasingly disillusioned about their ultimate triumph as he aged.

Loeb's early absorption of a materialistic perspective focused on the centrality of a mechanistic explanation that largely excluded the exercise of "free-will" on the part of humanity, although he was not always consistent on this point. In opposing mind-body dualism of the Cartesian and post-Cartesian variety he supported an ontological reductionist position. Indeed, in a letter to William James he projected a research program of epistemological or theory reduction when he explained behavior in terms of the "molecular or atomic structure of the protoplasm."[10] Because he believed that the goal of empirical science was to ascertain the causes, that is, antecedent determining conditions of behavior, this helped free him from dependence on "nonphysical" entities such as the conventional view of "consciousness."

Loeb often disclaimed any interest in or knowledge of philosophy, yet he engaged in antimetaphysical rhetoric; he held to the epistemological and ontological tenets of deterministic materialism—yet his primary focus was not on philosophic issues, but on the mechanisms for engineering control over the development of living organisms including human beings. He proposed nothing less than a wholesale reconstruction of the nature of biology and its future goals; this was the research agenda he hoped would enhance the claims of science and scientists over life. To illustrate the point, if physiologists could produce life artificially it might help persuade people to rely upon scientists to direct social change and guide future social development. Loeb believed, to reinforce the point, that artificial parthenogenesis, perhaps his greatest experimental achievement, might serve in the future as a model of science in which biologists would deliberately work to transform the natural order along

---

10. Loeb to William James, 10 June 1888, WJ AM 1092 (509).

more rational, efficient lines responsive to the continuing development of an engineering science which aimed at social control. As he once put it:

> We cannot allow any barrier to stand in the path of our complete *control* and thereby understanding of life phenomena. I believe that anyone will reach the same view who considers the control of natural phenomena as the essential problem of scientific research.[11]

Loeb's goal, then, was "engineering," that is, the control of existing and the production of new forms of behavior. This emphasis on "control" is seen repeatedly in Loeb's work, and of course was the hallmark of the writings of B. F. Skinner many years later. In a recent interesting analysis by Timothy D. Hachenberg, a strong case is made that the connection between the two, Loeb and Skinner, was more direct than generally assumed, not just historically but also intellectually; both scientists eschew the use of unseen and inaccessible processes, whether metaphysical or physiological, as the basis for a scientific explanation. Rather, both argued, scientific explanation is to be found in the ability to predict and control the phenomena under examination. Once prediction and control are at hand and demonstrated, then further hypothetical explanations become unnecessary. And both emphasized the value of applying scientific findings to human behavior.[12]

The most interesting questions raised by Loeb's work, however, from the perspective of the social scientist were the means and the extent to which he believed such achievements could be translated into "social engineering" of a collectivist nature. In short, what was the relationship between manipulation of the natural and social environment? Answering this question is the most difficult and problematic of all the political and social philosophical issues Loeb's life and work raise.

If the power could be found to reconstruct the living world according to the findings of empirical science, what political vehicles would it employ, that is, what role would partisan affiliation and politicking play? Loeb's writings were filled with denunciations of partisan political activity and although he sometimes supported "progressive" politicians and causes, he was mistrustful of the motives and behavior of both elected and appointed officials. Indeed, late in life he withdrew from electoral politics altogether,

---

11. Loeb, "Phenomena of Life," *Daily Californian* (6 March 1903), p. 25.

12. Hochenberg, Timothy D., "Jacques Loeb, B. F. Skinner, and the Legacy of Prediction and Control," *The Behavior Analyst*, 18 (1995), 225-36.

although he continued to engage in serious analysis and discussion of current political issues and affairs.

Nevertheless, most political scientists would probably view Loeb's political activism as unrealistic because of his inability to establish a means-ends continuum for the achievement of political goals. In his defense, however, it can be argued that he was probably more interested in changing the general climate of opinion in the long run than in influencing elites in the short run, although he sometimes attempted to do the latter also. He continued, of course, to believe that strong links existed between antimechanistic views in biology and racism, imperialism, ethnocentrism and militarism. But Phillip Pauly has argued that:

> a fundamental transformation . . . gradually took place in Loeb's outlook over the years for 1910-1918. He slowly shifted from broad hopes for biologists' present and future power to a belief that scientists could do only one, rather passive, thing: to look at nature and try to see the hidden mechanisms underlying biological processes. This change in emphasis from action to vision, from a practical positivism to an explicit epistemological reductionism, was accompanied in Loeb's mind by a different image of the social role of scientists; he no longer saw scientists as leaders in the transformation of the world, but as cloistral figures, removed from society, seeking pure knowledge. The result of this shift was a fundamental alteration in both Loeb's scientific identify and his research; after two decades as a leader in defining the science of biology, he became a chemist. By 1920 Loeb had become, in the words of his admirer Paul De Kruif, "the famous founder of philosophy of a mechanistic conception of life"; fictionalized as Max Gottieb in Sinclair Lewis's *Arrowsmith*, he became a central symbol of pure science in America during the years between the wars.[13]

It would be intriguing to further explore Loeb's apparent inclination at times to give privileged epistemological status and, consequently, to assign an elite political role to right-minded scientists like himself with scientistic-technocratic inclinations. Yet, in the final analysis Loeb did not really accept the efficacy of political action as the basic method of social transformation because he did not believe in the reason or good will of politicians or their independence from vested interests; nor would he have been willing to accept the domination of a scientific-technical elite.

---

13. Pauly, *Controlling Life*, p. 130.

Loeb was a scientist with a strong sense of his own philosophical roots; his outlook was decidedly progressive or leftist in view. He saw social structures as being, for the most part, the cause of suffering and social injustice; these social problems were, in turn, the result of political systems under the control of self-serving and/or incompetent politicians who were, in turn, under the control of an arrogant and greedy elite ruling class. He saw the solution in science for the findings of the sciences could be applied to human problems by an educated body of experts who would make day-to-day social decisions on the basis of scientific expertise. This basis for the management of society is to be built on the foundations of physics and chemistry and their application to the problems of biology and physiology and culminate in the extension of physico-chemical principles into the fields of psychology and even sociology. He well understood that scientific progress had not yet reached the level required for such a revolutionary advance in government decision-making mechanisms; but Loeb was convinced that scientific progress would continue in the directions necessary for such a "new era." He saw contemporary society as mired in a "Middle Ages" of greed and suffering, with science as the only solution. But obstacles, as he saw them, were the "greed and obstinacy of the ruling classes . . . and the greed and ignorance and stupidity of the 'lower classes'." He saw the ruling elite as clever self-serving manipulators and the masses as uneducated, easily manipulated and filled with cupidity in his more pessimistic moments.[14]

Nevertheless, at times Loeb's view of the possible future was a rather utopian world governed by Popper-Lynkeus's "engineering impulse," a place where racism, ethnocentrism and social injustice could be avoided through the judicious application of scientific principles. Democracy was not necessarily given up in favor of a scientific elite to replace the wealthy elite. Rather, in some fashion only vaguely alluded to by Loeb, a populace well educated in scientific principles would come to defer to expertise, perhaps by electing the experts. But, in the final analysis, like Lincoln, he did not think any human had the right to rule another without the other's consent.

Loeb was principled in his writing and in his behavior. He lent his name to a number of organizations founded in the name of social improvement. He also provided financial contributions and gave speeches in support of these causes. He provided scientific arguments against racist misinterpretations of biological principles

---

14. Loeb to Aristide Rieffel, 1 August 1919. In this letter Loeb also commented: "Do you not think I am right in trying to forget the world with its Simianism and that I try to find happiness to the pursuit of purely scientific work?"

and in favor of movements to reduce alcohol consumption. He was actively associated with the National Association for the Advancement of Colored People. He associated himself with prominent opponents of racism such as W. E. B. Dubois a prominent black leader, Oswald Garrison Villard, editor of *The Nation* and Thomas Hunt Morgan of Columbia University. In all of these activities he endeavored to draw from his vast scientific knowledge in order both to provide support for liberal causes and oppose the misapplication and misinterpretation of those who attempted to use scientific findings to support racism, ethnocentrism, elitism and war.

Loeb never completed his own research agenda; in fact, toward the end of his life he revealed flashes of pessimism about his own accomplishments, though these moments may well have been the result of the depressed mental state of an active man past his prime and acutely aware of his own ill health and general decline. Throughout his active, vigorous years, however, he held tenaciously to a few fundamental beliefs. First, that progress was being made in the development of a materialistic science of life; that, to this end, a number of life processes (tropisms in particular) had yielded themselves to a satisfactory mechanistic explanation. Ultimately all life processes, including life versus death and living versus nonliving matter, could be understood totally in terms of physico-chemical processes. He included mental processes, free will, and even consciousness in the list of phenomena to be understood in mechanistic terms. He acknowledged that many prominent scientists argued that the "truly psychical" would never be explained on the basis of physical chemistry, but Loeb was convinced to the contrary. However, he concluded that since the goal was far off and so much work remained to be done at a lower level, such a debate was premature. In any case, his laboratory experiments and the social and political ideals to which they helped give rise still await a behavioral technology and a political vehicle for their concrete realization.

ARCHIVES CONSULTED

COLLECTION	LOCATION
Clarence Ayres	Center for American History, University of Texas, Austin
Joseph Dorfman	Butler Library, Columbia University, New York
Irving Fisher	Yale University Library, New Haven, Connecticut
William Rainey Harper	Regenstein Library, University of Chicago, Chicago, Illinois
David S. Jordan	Stanford University Archives, Cecil H. Green Library, Stanford, California
Jacques Loeb	Library of Congress, Manuscript Division, Washington, D.C.
George H. Mead	Regenstein Library, University of Chicago, Chicago, Illinois
Wesley C. Mitchell	Butler Library, Columbia University, New York
Thorstein Veblen	Wisconsin State Historical Society, Madison University Library, Carleton College, Northfield, Minnesota

BIBLIOGRAPHY

Ayres, C.E. "Veblen's Theory of Instincts" in Dowd Douglas, Ed. *Thorstein Veblen: A Critical Reappraisal.* Ithaca, N.Y., Cornell University Press, 1958.

Bergson, Henri. *Creative Evolution.* Arthur Mitchell, trans, Lanham, Maryland: University Press ofAmerica, 1984. c1911.

Boring, E.G. "The Influence of Evolutionary Theory Upon American Psychological Thought" in Persons, Stow (ed.) *Evolutionary Thought in America.* New York: Archon Books, 1968.

Campbell, James. *The Community Reconstructs: The Meaning of Pragmatic Social Thought.* Urbana: University of Illinois Press, 1992.

Coats, A.W. "The Influence of Veblen's Methodology." *Journal of Political Economy,* 62 (1954): 529-37.

Cohen, Seymour S. "Balancing Science and History: A Problem of Scientific Biography." *History and Philosophy of the Life Sciences,* 8 (1986): 121-28.

_____. "Some Struggles of Jacques Loeb, Albert Mathews and Ernest Just at the Marine Biological Laboratory," *Biological Bulletin,* 168 (Supplement) (1985): 127-36.

Commager, Henry Steele. *The American Mind.* New Haven: Yale University Press, 1950.

Commons, John R. *Institutional Economics,* Vol. II. Madison: University of Wisconsin Press, 1961.

Diggins, John P. *The Bard of Savagery: Thorstein Veblen and Modern Social Theory.* New York: The Seabury Press, 1978.

Dobriansky, Lev E. *Veblenism: A New Critique.* Washington D.C.: Public Affairs Press, 1957.

Dorfman, Joseph. *Thorstein Veblen and His America.* New York: Viking Press, 1934.

Downes, William H. "Jacques Loeb" in Malone, Dumas (ed.) *Dictionary of American Biography.* New York: Charles Scribner's Sons, 1933.

169

_____. "Jacques Loeb: Mechanist." *Century Magazine,* 109 (1924): 374-83.

Flexner, Abraham. *Remember: The Autobiography of Abraham Flexner.* New York: Simon and Schuster, Inc., 1940.

Goudge, T. A. "Jacques Loeb" in Edwards, Paul (ed.) *The Encyclopedia of Philosophy.* New York: Macmillan Company and Free Press, 1967.

Grunchy, Allan G. *Modern Economic Thought: The American Contribution.* New York: Prentice-Hall, 1947.

Hachenberg, Timothy D. "Jacques Loeb, B. F. Skinner, and the Legacy of Prediction and Control." *The Behavior Analyst,* 18 (1995): 225-36.

James, William. *Principles of Psychology.* New York: Holt, 1890.

_____. *The Correspondence of William James.* Skrupskelis, I. K. and Berkeley, E. M. (eds.) Charlottesville: University Press of Virginia, 1992.

Kay, Lily E. *The Molecular Vision of Life: Caltech, The Rockefeller Foundation and the Rise of the New Biology.* New York: Oxford University Press, 1993.

Kuznick, Peter J. *Beyond the Laboratory: Scientists as Political Activists in the 1930s.* Chicago: University of Chicago Press, 1987.

Lewis, Sinclair. *Arrowsmith.* New York: Harcourt, Brace, 1924.

Loeb, Jacques. "Biology and War." *Science,* 26 (1917): 74-5.

_____. *Comparative Physiology of the Brain and Comparative Psychology.* New York: G.P. Putman's Sons, 1900.

_____. *The Dynamics of Living Matter.* New York: Macmillan, 1906.

_____. *Forced Movements, Tropisms, and Animal Conduct.* Monographs on Experimental Biology, vol. 1. Philadelphia: J.B. Lippincott, 1918.

_____. "Freedom of the Will and War." *New Review,* 2 (1914): 631-36.

_____. *The Mechanistic Conception of Life: Biological Essays.* Chicago: University of Chicago Press, 1912.

_____. "Mechanistic Science and Metaphysical Romance." *Yale Review*, 4 (1915): 768-69.

_____. *The Organism as a Whole*. New York and London: G.P. Putnam's Sons, 1916.

_____. "Phenomena of Life." *Daily Californian* (6 March 1903) 25.

_____. *Proteins and the Theory of Colloidal Behavior*. New York: McGrawHill, 1924.

_____. "The Significance of Tropisms for Psychology." *The Popular Science Monthly*, 79 (August 1911): 122.

Manning, Kenneth R. *Black Apollo of Science: The Life of Ernest Everett Just*. New York: Oxford University Press, 1983.

McDougall, William. *Introduction to Social Psychology*. London: Methuen, 1908.

Mitchell, Wesley C. (ed.) *What Veblen Taught*. New York: Augustus M. Kelley, 1964.

Moorehead, Caroline. *Bertrand Russell: A Life*. New York: Viking Press, 1988.

Morgan, C. Lloyd. *Habit and Instinct*. London: Arnold, 1896.

_____. *An Introduction to Comparative Psychology*. London: Walter Scott, 1894.

Pauly, Phillip J. *Controlling Life: Jacques Loeb and the Engineering Ideal in Biology*. New York: Oxford University Press, 1987.

Riesman, David. *Thorstein Veblen: A Critical Interpretation*. New York: Charles Scribner's Sons, 1960.

Rosenberg, Bernard. (ed.) *Thorstein Veblen*. New York: Thomas Y. Crowell, 1963.

Ryan, Allan. *Bertrand Russell: A Political Life*. New York: Hill and Wang, 1988.

Sibley, Mulford. "Pacifism." *International Encyclopedia of the Social Sciences*, David Sills, ed., Vol. II. New York: Macmillan Company and Free Press, 1968.

Spillman, Jutta and Luther Spillman, "The Rise and Fall of Hugo Münsterberg." *Journal of the History of the Behavioral Sciences*, 29

(1993): 322-38.

Tilman, Rick. *Thorstein Veblen and His Critics, 1891-1963: Conservative, Liberal and Radical Perspectives.* Princeton: Princeton University Press, 1992.

Tobey, Ronald C. *The American Ideology of National Science, 1919-1930.* Pittsburgh: University of Pittsburgh Press, 1971.

Tool, Marc, *Essays in Social Value Theory.* Armonk, N.Y.: M.E. Sharpe, 1986.

Veblen, Thorstein. *Absentee Ownerships.* Boston: Beacon Press, 1967.

_____. *The Instinct of Workmanship.* New York: B.W. Huebsch, 1914.

_____. *Imperial Germany and the Industrial Revolution.* New York: Macmillian, 1915.

_____. *The Nature of Peace.* New York: Macmillian, 1917.

_____. *The Higher Learning in America.* New York: B. W. Huebsch, 1918.

_____. *The Place of Science in Modern Civilization.* New York: Viking Press, 1930.

_____. *The Theory of the Leisure Class.* New York: Macmillan, 1899.

Weissman, Gerald. *The Woods Hole Cantata: Essays on Science.* New York: Dodd and Mead, 1985.

Woodward, C. Van. *The Strange Career of Jim Crow.* New York: Oxford University Press, 1966.

Zanine, Louis J. *Mechanism and Mysticism: The Influence of Science on the Thought and Work of Theodore Dreiser.* Philadelphia: University of Pennsylvania Press, 1993.

INDEX

175

psychophysics, 4

racism, 2, 20-21, 40, 102-3, 119, 123-37, 141, 148, 159, 165-66
reductionism, 4-5, 16, 28, 30, 93, 95, 101, 118, 159, 162
religion, 2, 12-13, 28, 32, 35, 67-68, 75-79, 103, 156
Richet, Charles, 52
Rieffel, Aristide, 72, 150, 165
Rignano, Eugenio, 28
Robertson, Thornburn Brailsford, 49
Rockefeller Institute for Medical Research, 7, 26, 65-66, 70, 72, 84, 120, 132-33, 137-38, 157
Rockefeller, John D., Jr., 77
Roosevelt, Franklin D., 150
Roosevelt, Theodore, 10, 29, 42, 85-88, 146, 149
Roux, William, 149
Rüdinger, Nikolaus, 3
Rush Medical College, 7
Russell, Bertrand, 88, 89, 91
Rutherford, Ernest, 39, 82, 84, 123, 143

Sachs, Julius, 4, 8
Salisbury, Lord, 86
Sanger, Margaret, 66
Sarton, George, 81, 93
Schopenhauer, Artur, 2
Schull, A. Franklin, 83, 127
science, 1, 7, 12-13, 29-30, 33, 36, 57-58, 77-87, 94, 100, 119, 130, 144-46, 150, 152-59
secular humanism, 1, 33, 65, 75-79, 88
Shaw, Bernard, 42, 62
Shelly, Rebecca, 74
Sibley, Mulford, 53-54
Sinclair, Upton, 93
Skeel, R.E., 76
Skinner, B.F., 7, 152, 163
Small, Albion, 6
Smith, Hugh, 82-83
Social Reform, 2, 5-6, 23
Spinoza, Baruch, 2
Springarn, J.E., 148, 150
Steinmetz, Charles, 73
Stieglitz, Julius, 55
Strassburg, University of, 3, 6
Sunday, Billy, 68, 76-77

Taylor, George C., 35-36
Thomson, John Authur, 35, 82
Titchener, E.B., 36-37
Tobey, Ronald, 157, 159-60
von Treitschke, Heinrich, 81, 125
tropisms, 4-5, 8, 12, 96-100, 104-7, 110, 118, 144, 155, 166
Tufts, James Hayden, 78

Veblen, Thorstein, 10, 13, 23, 54-55, 93-121, 159
Viereck, George S., 87
Villard, Oswald Garrison, 10, 30, 93, 127, 166
vitalism, 2, 8-9, 13-14, 22-33, 35, 57-58, 94-95, 98, 100, 112-13
vivisection, 75
Voit, Carl, 3
Voltaire, Francois Marie Arouet de, 11
Vries, Hugo de, 46

Walling, William English, 26, 41, 48, 73-74, 93
Warbasse, Dr. James P., 52
Warburg, Otto, 59
Wasteneys, Hardolph, 26, 151
Watson, James D., 14
Watson, John B., 7, 10, 93, 96
Weissman, Gerald, 6, 102
Weizmann, Chaim, 138-39
Wells, H.G., 130
Wheeler, Benjamin Ide, 130
Whitman, Charles Otis, 6
Wilhelm II, Emperor, 40
Wilson, Woodrow, 10, 37, 43-45, 54, 56, 62, 88, 145-46, 149-50
Wodsedaleh, J.E., 126
Wood, L. Hollingsworth, 53, 60
Wurtzburg, University of, 4, 6

Zanine, Louis J., 8
Zuntz, Nathan, 3
Zionism, 137-41